Stylish Skirts

23 Easy-to-Sew Skirts to Flatter Every Figure

Sato Watanabe

TUTTLE Publishing

Tokyo | Rutland, Vermont | Singapore

Sew straight for beautiful skirts everyday and feminine styles to make in exactly your size.

—Sato Watanabe

Contents

Lace and Embroidery

(A) Embroidered Skirt with Gathered Waist and Lace Hem

A simple gathered skirt is brought to life with a regular pattern of embroidery. Drawing in construction marks is easy, as only straight lines are needed. The leaf-like embroidery uses three colors of thread. Torchon lace along the hem makes the skirt even sweeter.

how to make→page 34-35

Tape and Stitching

Ⓑ 12-panel Skirt with Embroidery and Tape Decoration

This neat A-line skirt is created from twelve trapezoid panels. Lines of tape in varying widths and fabrics add a sense of rhythm, while latticework embroidery along the hem lends a couture edge. For a stylish look, use the same color for the tape and the embroidery.

how to make→page 36-37

A-line

ⓒ White Twill A-line Skirt

A wide hem falls from the straight, clean silhouette on this A-line skirt. It has a buttoned opening on the front right and pockets on the back, creating a pleasing appearance from behind as well as in front. Pair it with a striped top for a nautical look.

how to make→page 38-41

Slub Denim

D Slub Denim Wrap-style Panel Skirt

This wrap-style skirt is accented by the panel attached to the front right, which has a longer hem than the rest of the garment. I think it would look cool worn on the hips in a rough kind of style. It could also be made into a longer version by extending the sides in a straight line.

how to make→page 42-43

Russel Lace

Ⓔ Russel Lace Gored Skirt

This unashamedly feminine lace skirt is lined with sheeting to give it body. Its flattering line is neat around the hips, with gores beginning below the hips and flaring out to a full hemline. The pink trim in a separate fabric at the waist adds a pretty accent.

how to make→page 44-45

Irregular Hem

 F Skirt with Lace-trimmed Irregular Hem

There is a strong sense of design to this skirt, which is made from a square piece of material. Black lace attractively accents the movement of the hem when the skirt is worn, while darts in the yoke create a snug fit on the hips. It's also possible to make by omitting the darts in the yoke and using elastic around the waist instead.

how to make→page 46-47

Box Pleats

G Striped Skirt with Box Pleats

Here the classic box pleat skirt is worked in striped linen, with the stripes running vertically on the inner part of the pleats for contrast. As a favorite for spring and summer, this piece is a sure thing, but try it in a different fabric for fall and winter. It would also look great with the inner part of the pleats made in a different fabric.

how to make→page 48-51

Frill

H Tiered-look Frill Skirt

Frills are layered onto a gathered-waist skirt, creating a tiered look. Variations in the frills' length and width add a sense of movement to the design. Stitch along the edges of the frills using a light colored thread to subtly emphasize the random lines of this design.

how to make→page 52-53

Escargot

1 Long Jacquard "Escargot" Skirt with Straight Hem Panel

The silhouette of this skirt widens towards the hem, which hangs straight. This is achieved by joining trapezoid shapes on the diagonal and attaching a straight hem panel. The end result looks a bit like a snail shell. This skirt would look cute with lace or some other decoration along the skirt panel seams too. The zip is inserted in line with the diagonal seams.

how to make→page 54-55

Irregular Gathering

J Skirt with Irregular Gathering

This skirt has gathering at irregular intervals. At the center back, the gathering is lower than at the front for a change of focus. The waist cord can be tied at the side for a different look. Their versatility is one of the great things about skirts sewn using straight lines.

how to make→page 56-57

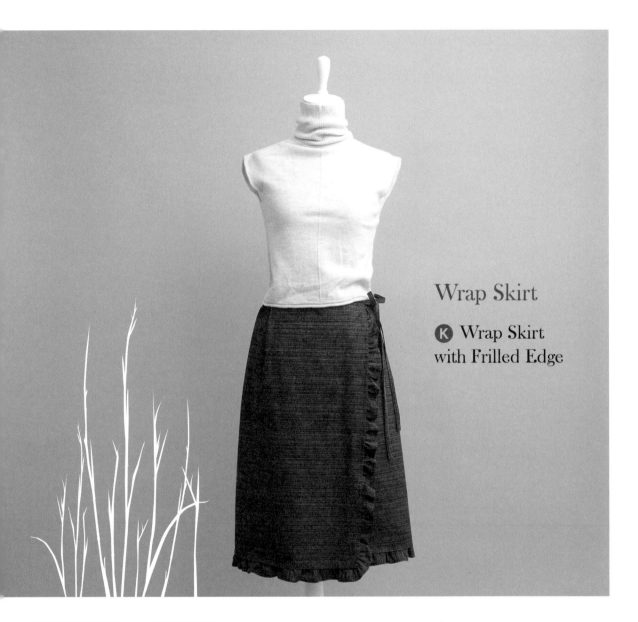

Wrap Skirt

K Wrap Skirt with Frilled Edge

By adding darts around the waist, a skirt drafted and sewn with straight lines becomes more three-dimensional. A gathered frill has been added along the front edge and hem for a sweet touch.

how to make→page 58-59

Pleated Skirt

 ⓛ Trapezoid Skirt with Line Detail

This trapezoid pattern confirms how pleats can create a pleasing silhouette. Joining pleats to panels means that the hem doesn't flare out too much.
A line of white tape attached near the hemline sharpens the look.
Enjoy a grown-up, nautical style in this skirt that's much more than plain old navy and white.

how to make→page 60-62

Denim Skirt

Ⓜ Denim Skirt with Patch Pocket

When using denim, I think a simple design is desirable. This skirt has seams positioned at the front right and center back, and the small patch pocket at the front and larger version at the back add subtle details. Waist darts have been added to flatter the hip area.

how to make→page 64-67

Tuck & Lace

N Tucked and Gathered Cotton Skirt

In pink and trimmed with lace, this skirt embodies loveliness. Brown grosgrain ribbon has been threaded through the eyelet lace trim, perhaps giving something of a streamlining effect. Use a heavy material to tone down the volume and transform the skirt into a more elegant design.

how to make→page 68-69

Tweed

◉ Tweed Skirt with Panel Detail

This slightly avant-garde skirt has been created by joining squares and triangles of fabric. It hangs smoothly at the back, but is more expressive in the front. Have fun styling it with boots that peek out from under the hem. It would look cute made in denim too.

how to make→page 70-73

Balloon Skirt

Ⓟ Long Balloon Skirt

The secret to creating a balloon skirt lies in the lining. By gathering the voluminous hem of the outer layer and stitching it to a closer-fitting lining, the material draws up to form a pleasant balloon hemline. Tucks at the waistline give it a neat fit.

how to make→page 74-79

Black Balloon

ⓠ Black Balloon Skirt

This mid-length balloon skirt suits both dressed-up and more casual outfits. Use a stiff fabric to create a more voluminous silhouette. A cord is used around the waist, making for flexible sizing.

how to make→page 74-79

Shirring

ℝ Skirt with Shirred Yoke and Lace Belt

This skirt has evenly-spaced shirring around the waist and hips. It's based on a gathered skirt but the shirring means it fits well around the hips. The skirt has a slight bell shape, and the waist belt uses the same lace as the trim around the hem.

how to make→page 80-81

Linen

Linen Skirt with Cargo Pockets

I created this skirt in linen because even if it gets wrinkled, it's still stylish. With cargo pockets and an A-line shape, this versatile piece works for casual looks but still looks cool. Here it's worn as a hip-hanger but it would be cute drawn in and worn on the waist.

how to make→page 82-83

Stitch and Tuck

T Embroidered Skirt with Horizontal Tuck Pattern

Even though it's made from simple fabric, with a little effort—embroidery between the tucks—this skirt becomes something special. Making the tucks requires a bit of work, but think of how much satisfaction you'll get from it.

how to make→page 84-85

Eight Buttons

Ⓤ Eight-button Skirt with Horizontal Stripe Sections

Fabric in three different colors has been used to create horizontal panels in this skirt. Why not try linen in natural shades for a summer version or warm hues in flannel for a winter skirt? Choose buttons in a different color from the fabric to make them stand out.

how to make→page 86-87

Three Colors

Ⓥ 18-panel Skirt in Three Colors

This skirt is made from trapezoid shapes in three colors. Using six pieces of each color, there are 18 panels in all. Some of the seams joining the panels are turned inside out in the manner of French seams. I think adding irregularity such as this gives a simple design some personality. The color combination is up to you!

how to make→page 88-89

Irregular Flare

Ⓦ Eight-panel Irregular Flare Skirt in Lace

At its core, this is a generously proportioned eight-panel skirt, but I've added an extra element by using different fabrics within each panel. The various textures of the different black fabrics make the skirt visually interesting, and the zipper sewn on the outside gives it plenty of character.

how to make→page 90-93

Notes on Linings

C White twill A-line skirt

The lining for the A-line skirt is made from the same pattern as the skirt itself. For skirts such as this, which has a facing, the lining is made without the facing section. There is no seam allowance for the hem, which is made by folding up ⅝-⅞ in (1.5-2cm) of material twice and stitching it into place. This creates a hem about ⅞-1¼ in (2-3cm) shorter than the skirt itself.

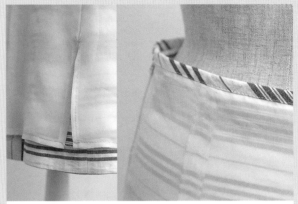

G Striped skirt with box pleats

The box pleat skirt also has an A-line silhouette. The lining is made using the same pattern as the skirt but without the pleated section. The skirt has some fullness due to the box pleats, so slits have been made up the sides of the lining to allow it to follow the fall of the skirt. For a 25½-in (65cm) long skirt, slits of about 7⅞-8 in (20cm) should be fine.

P, Q Balloon skirts

For gathered or balloon skirts where there is a lot of fabric, it's best to use an A-line pattern for the lining. To allow some leeway, there are tucks at the waist. When making a balloon skirt, the hems of the skirt and the lining are sewn together, but for the lining in a regular gathered skirt, fold the hem up three times as per C above.

W Eight-panel irregular flare skirt in lace

For a flared skirt without too much fullness, it's fine to make the lining from the same pattern as the skirt itself. Joining pattern pieces allows the lining to be made from four panels rather than eight. For a skirt with a full hem, slits on the side are not necessary although you can create them if you wish. Cut the lining pieces to the same length as the skirt pieces without a hem allowance and turn up 1¼ in (3cm) to create the hem.

Tips for Making Better Skirts

Skirts like the A-line which have a trapezoid silhouette have been made as hip-hangers, so they have slightly large waists. Wear them on your hips, or bring them up to your true waistline and draw them in with a belt so that they fit snugly.

Trapezoid-shaped skirts are cool worn on the hips, and garments fitted properly on the hip bones create a smooth, sleek line.

No two figures are the same. The skirt you make won't necessarily fit perfectly. For those of you who are well-rounded in the waist-hip area, shorten the length between waist and hip when drawing up your pattern. This will inevitably give you more volume at the hem, but will mean other areas are no longer too tight. Otherwise, create a slight curve in the pattern rather than using straight lines to connect waist to hips. When you draft your pattern, add $1\frac{1}{4}$-$1\frac{5}{8}$ in (3-4cm) for a looser fit to the waist (W) and hips (H). In other words, create the pattern with the "finished measurements" as a guide for the waist (W) and hips (H). Skirt lengths are up to you, as you can lengthen or shorten the pattern wherever you like. If you have a skirt in your wardrobe that is the right length, use it as a guide when creating the skirts in this book.

Please note that measurements are given in both inches and metrics. Using metrics measurements if possible will give you a more precise cut, fit and drape.

In the case of fabric/tape widths and zipper lengths, we have attempted to provide inch measurements that conform to US standard sizes.

For some projects, the detailed steps may be presented nonsequentially. Please review all steps and corresponding diagrams before proceeding with your project.

ⓐ Embroidered Skirt with Gathered Waist and Lace Hem (photo→p.4)

MATERIALS

Fabric—slub cotton 44 in (106cm) wide x 1⅔ yd (1.5m)
Iron-on interfacing—⅞ in (2cm) x 9 in (23cm)
8 in (20cm) zipper x 1
Waistband stiffening— 1⅛ in (3cm) wide x
   [your waist measurement + 1⅛ in (3cm)]
Lace—⅞ in (2cm) wide x 2¼ yd (2m)
Skirt hook and bar
One snap fastener
Embroidery thread – white, orange, brown

SEWING STEPS

1. Sew left side and attach zipper
2. Sew right side and open out seam
3. Attach waistband
4. Attach lace to hem
5. Attach skirt hook and bar
6. Embroider pattern

● Drafting and cutting out

(Seam allowances are all ⅜in (1cm))

3. Attach belt

① Mark symbols on fabric

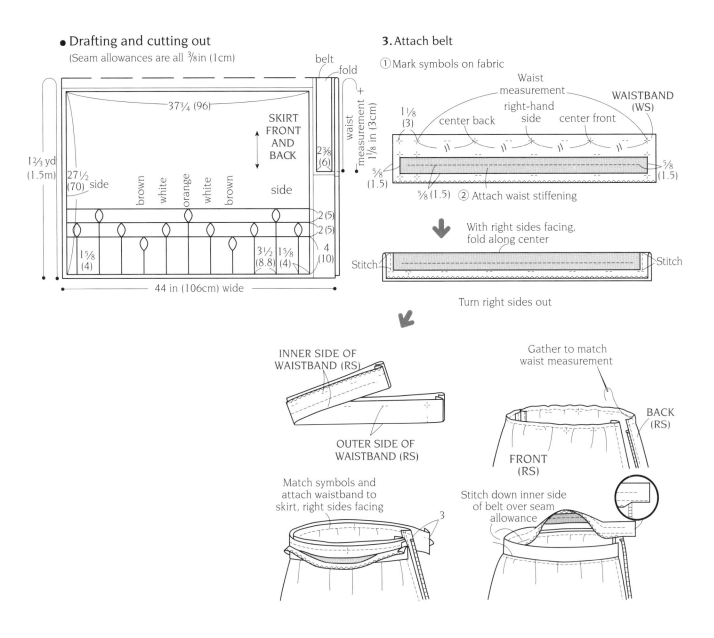

② Attach waist stiffening

With right sides facing, fold along center

Turn right sides out

INNER SIDE OF WAISTBAND (RS)

OUTER SIDE OF WAISTBAND (RS)

Match symbols and attach waistband to skirt, right sides facing

Gather to match waist measurement

BACK (RS)

FRONT (RS)

Stitch down inner side of belt over seam allowance

1.Sew left side seam, attach zipper

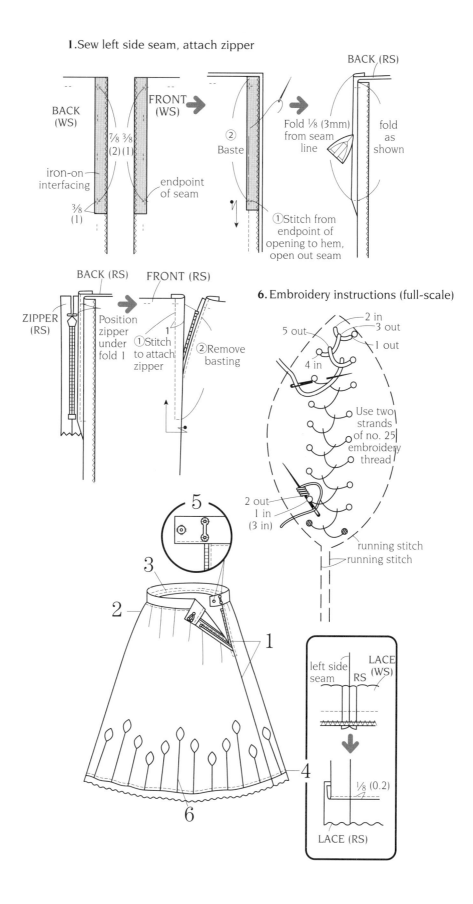

BACK (WS)

iron-on interfacing

7/8 3/8
(2)(1)

3/8
(1)

endpoint of seam

FRONT (WS) →

② Baste

① Stitch from endpoint of opening to hem, open out seam

Fold 1/8 (3mm) from seam line →

BACK (RS)

fold as shown

BACK (RS) FRONT (RS)

ZIPPER (RS)

Position zipper under fold 1

① Stitch to attach zipper

② Remove basting

6. Embroidery instructions (full-scale)

5 out
2 in
3 out
1 out
4 in

Use two strands of no. 25 embroidery thread

2 out
1 in
(3 in)

running stitch
running stitch

left side seam
LACE (WS)
RS

1/8 (0.2)

LACE (RS)

Ⓑ 12-panel Skirt with Embroidery and Tape Decoration (photo→p.5)

MATERIALS

Fabric—plain gray fabric 44 in (110cm) wide x 2½ yd (2.3m)
Iron-on interfacing—⅞ in (2cm) x9 in (22cm)
1 x invisible zipper, 9 in (22cm) long
Hook and eye
Organza tape 1 in (2.5cm) x 1½ yd (1.4m)
Leather cord ³⁄₁₆ (0.4cm) wide x 1¾ yd (1m)
Embroidery thread—black

SEWING STEPS

1. Join 12 panels together
2. Sew left side to opening and insert invisible zipper (see p76)
3. Attach waistband
4. Create hem (see p67)
5. Attach tape
6. Embroider hem
7. Attach hook and eye (see p63)

• Drafting

Drafting order

①Draft rectangle (shaded section of diagram)
②Draft hem
③At midpoint of hip, draft up 7 in (18cm) to create waist
④Join P and Q with a straight line
⑤Draft in a naturally curved line from Q to R

1.Join 12 panels

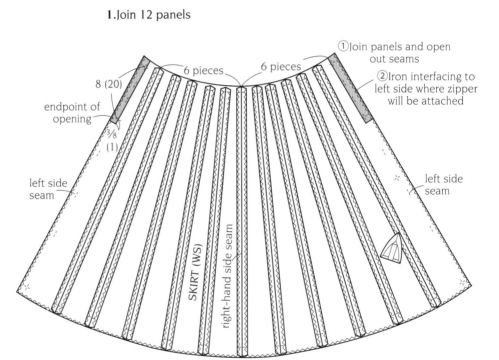

①Join panels and open out seams

②Iron interfacing to left side where zipper will be attached

6 pieces   6 pieces

8 (20)

endpoint of opening

³⁄₈ (1)

left side seam

left side seam

SKIRT (WS)

right-hand side seam

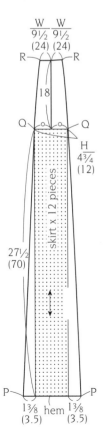

W 9½ (24)   W 9½ (24)

R ⌒⌒ R

18

Q ⌒⌒⌒ Q

H 4¾ (12)

skirt x 12 pieces

27½ (70)

P — P

1⅜ (3.5)   hem   1⅜ (3.5)

• Cutting layout

Figures inside brackets show seam allowances.
Where not indicated, allow ⅜ in (1cm).

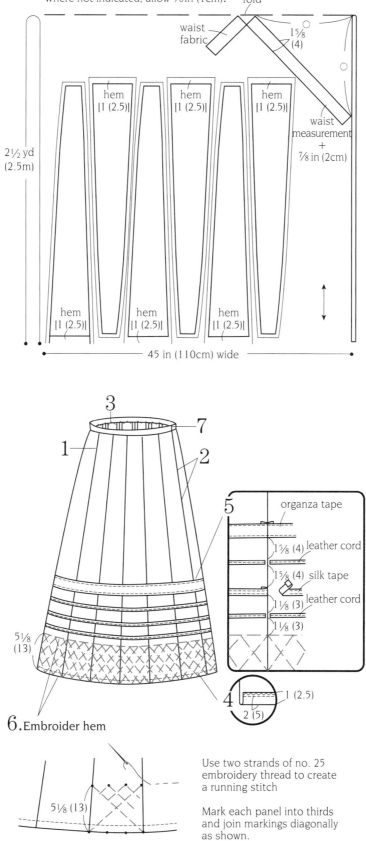

fold

waist fabric

1⅝ (4)

waist measurement
+
⅞ in (2cm)

2½ yd (2.5m)

hem [1 (2.5)]

hem [1 (2.5)]

hem [1 (2.5)]

hem [1 (2.5)]

hem [1 (2.5)]

hem [1 (2.5)]

45 in (110cm) wide

3
7
1
2
5

organza tape

1⅝ (4) leather cord

1⅝ (4) silk tape

1⅛ (3) leather cord

1⅛ (3)

5⅛ (13)

4
1 (2.5)
2 (5)

6. Embroider hem

5⅛ (13)

Use two strands of no. 25 embroidery thread to create a running stitch

Mark each panel into thirds and join markings diagonally as shown.

38

❸ White Twill A-line Skirt (photo→p.6-7)

MATERIALS

Fabric—twill 56 in (142cm) wide x 2¼ yd (2m)
Lining—Bemberg 36 in (92cm) x 1⅞ yd (1.7m)
Iron-on interfacing—24 in (60cm) x 16 in (40cm)
Buttons—8 at 1 in (2.3cm) diameter; 2 at ¾ in (1.8cm) diameter

SEWING STEPS

1. Attach pockets
2. Sew front left seam and stitch on outer side of fabric
3. Sew side seams to mark at waist
4. Attach facing (see p87)
5. Sew front right seam and stitch on outer side of fabric
6. Create hem (see p67)
7. Attach lining
8. Make buttonholes and attach buttons (see p63)

● Drafting

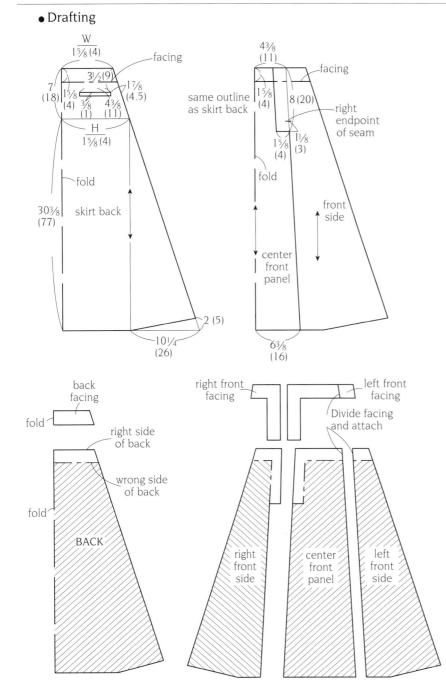

Lining pattern is created by removing facing sections from outer skirt pattern

1.Attach pockets

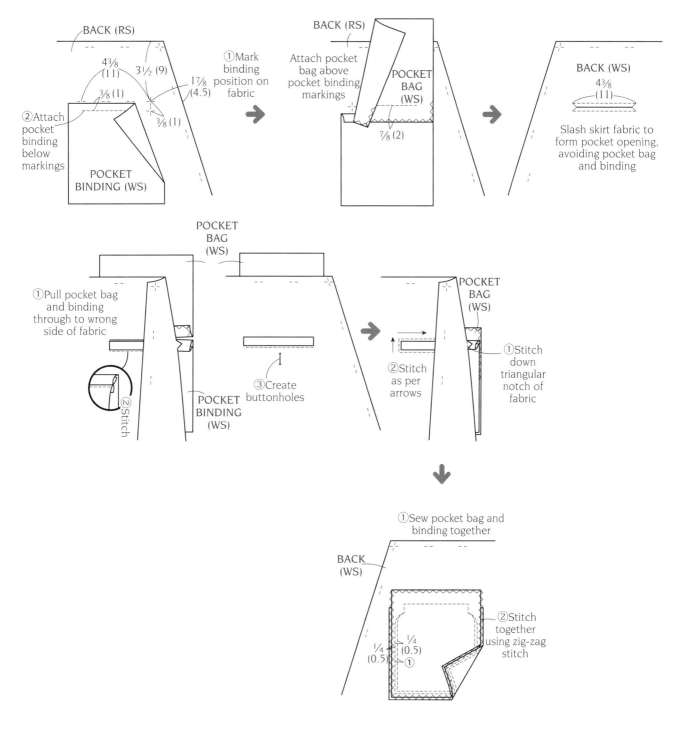

BACK (RS)

4⅜ (11)   3½ (9)

⅜ (1)   1⅞ (4.5)

⅜ (1)

①Mark binding position on fabric

②Attach pocket binding below markings

POCKET BINDING (WS)

BACK (RS)

Attach pocket bag above pocket binding markings

POCKET BAG (WS)

⅞ (2)

BACK (WS)

4⅜ (11)

Slash skirt fabric to form pocket opening, avoiding pocket bag and binding

POCKET BAG (WS)

①Pull pocket bag and binding through to wrong side of fabric

②Stitch

POCKET BINDING (WS)

③Create buttonholes

②Stitch as per arrows

POCKET BAG (WS)

①Stitch down triangular notch of fabric

①Sew pocket bag and binding together

BACK (WS)

¼ (0.5)
¼ (0.5)
①

②Stitch together using zig-zag stitch

40

● Cutting layout (skirt)

Figures inside brackets show seam allowances. Where not indicated, allow ⅜ in (1cm).

5. Sew right front seam and topstitch

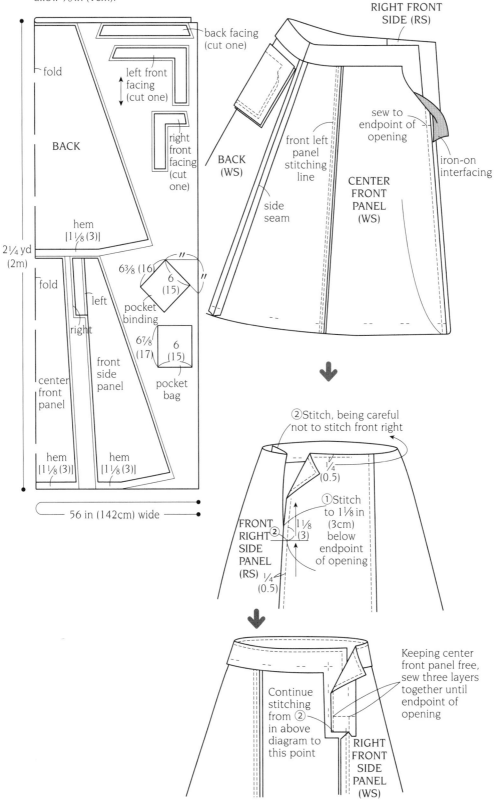

RIGHT FRONT SIDE (RS)

back facing (cut one)

fold

left front facing (cut one)

right front facing (cut one)

BACK

BACK (WS)

front left panel stitching line

side seam

sew to endpoint of opening

iron-on interfacing

CENTER FRONT PANEL (WS)

hem [1⅛ (3)]

2¼ yd (2m)

6⅜ (16)

6 (15)

fold

left

right

pocket binding

6⅞ (17)

6 (15)

center front panel

front side panel

pocket bag

hem [1⅛ (3)]

hem [1⅛ (3)]

56 in (142cm) wide

② Stitch, being careful not to stitch front right

¼ (0.5)

① Stitch to 1⅛ in (3cm) below endpoint of opening

FRONT RIGHT SIDE PANEL (RS)

1⅛ (3)

②

¼ (0.5)

Keeping center front panel free, sew three layers together until endpoint of opening

Continue stitching from ② in above diagram to this point

RIGHT FRONT SIDE PANEL (WS)

7.Attach lining

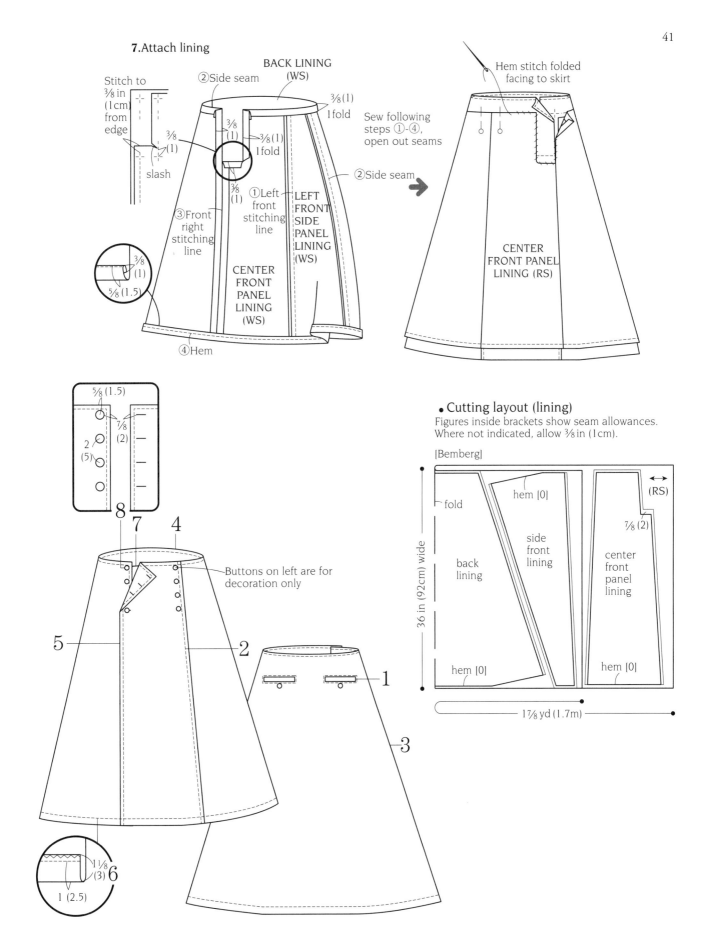

Stitch to ³⁄₈ in (1cm) from edge

slash

³⁄₈ (1)

②Side seam

BACK LINING (WS)

³⁄₈ (1) 1 fold

Sew following steps ①-④, open out seams

②Side seam

Hem stitch folded facing to skirt

CENTER FRONT PANEL LINING (RS)

③Front right stitching line

①Left front stitching line

LEFT FRONT SIDE PANEL LINING (WS)

CENTER FRONT PANEL LINING (WS)

³⁄₈ (1)
⁵⁄₈ (1.5)

④Hem

⁵⁄₈ (1.5)
⁷⁄₈ (2)
2 (5)

Buttons on left are for decoration only

1 ¹⁄₈ (3)
1 (2.5)

• Cutting layout (lining)
Figures inside brackets show seam allowances. Where not indicated, allow ³⁄₈ in (1cm).

[Bemberg]

fold
hem [0]
back lining
side front lining
center front panel lining
⁷⁄₈ (2)
(RS)
hem [0]
hem [0]

36 in (92cm) wide

1 ⁷⁄₈ yd (1.7m)

D Slub Denim Wrap-style Denim Skirt (photo→p.6-7)

MATERIALS
Fabric–yarn-dyed slub denim 45 in (114cm) wide x 1⅔ yd (1.5m)
Iron-on interfacing–7⅞ in (20cm) x 20 in (50cm)
1 x invisible zipper 9 in (22cm) long
Hook and eye
Leather cord–⅜ in (1cm) wide x 1¾ yd (1.6m)

SEWING STEPS
1. Sew left side until opening and insert zipper (see p76)
2. Neaten hem, front edge and waist of front panel by folding three times and stitching in place. Attach to right of skirt.
3. Attach interfacing to waist
4. Create hem. Position and attach leather cord as shown.
5. Attach hook and eye (see p63)

● Drafting

2. Attach front panel

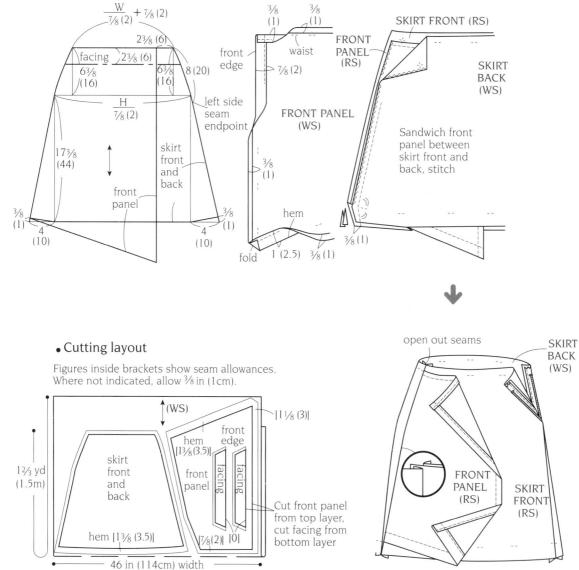

● Cutting layout

Figures inside brackets show seam allowances.
Where not indicated, allow ⅜ in (1cm).

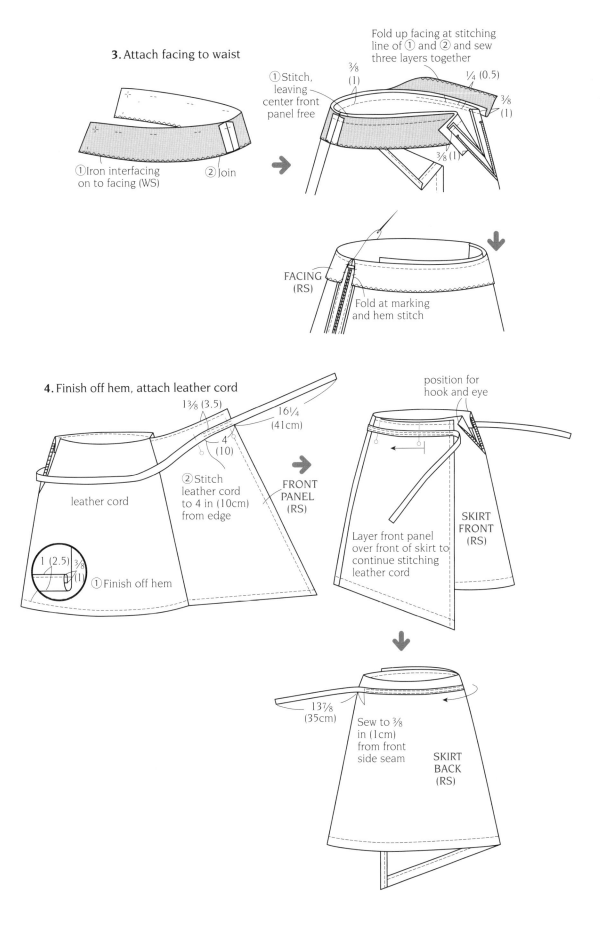

3. Attach facing to waist

① Iron interfacing on to facing (WS)
② Join

① Stitch, leaving center front panel free

Fold up facing at stitching line of ① and ② and sew three layers together

⅜ (1)   ¼ (0.5)   ⅜ (1)

⅜ (1)

FACING (RS)

Fold at marking and hem stitch

4. Finish off hem, attach leather cord

1⅜ (3.5)   16¼ (41cm)

4 (10)

② Stitch leather cord to 4 in (10cm) from edge

FRONT PANEL (RS)

leather cord

1 (2.5)   ⅜ (1)

① Finish off hem

position for hook and eye

Layer front panel over front of skirt to continue stitching leather cord

SKIRT FRONT (RS)

13⅞ (35cm)

Sew to ⅜ in (1cm) from front side seam

SKIRT BACK (RS)

❸ Russel Lace Gored Skirt (photo→p.8)

MATERIALS

Fabric—Russel lace 44 in (110cm) wide x 2½ yd (2.3m)
Sheeting (for underskirt) 44 in (110cm) x 2½ yd (2.3m)
Plain pink fabric (for waistband) 36 in (90cm) x ⅔ yd (0.6m)
1 x invisible zipper, 9 in (22cm) long
Hook and eye

SEWING STEPS

1. Sew underskirt and skirt pieces together
2. Sew left side and create gores
3. Insert zipper (see p76)
4. Join remaining panels and complete main part of skirt
5. Attach waistband (see 50)
6. Create hem (see p67)

• Drafting

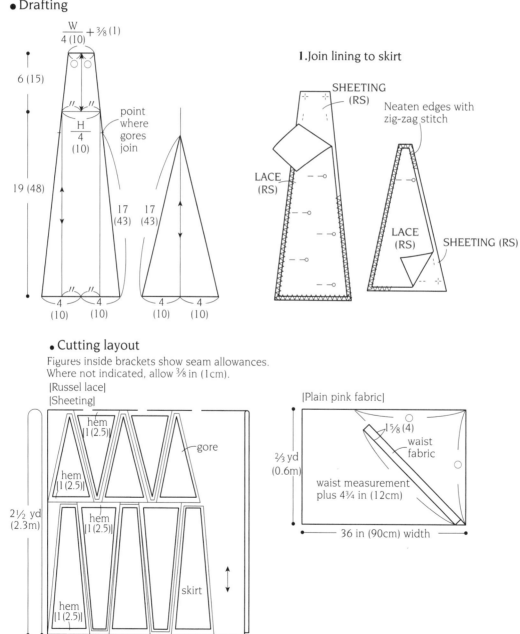

1.Join lining to skirt

$$\frac{W}{4}(10) + \frac{3}{8}(1)$$

6 (15)

$$\frac{H}{4}(10)$$

point where gores join

19 (48)

17 (43)   17 (43)

4 (10)   4 (10)   4 (10)   4 (10)

SHEETING (RS)

Neaten edges with zig-zag stitch

LACE (RS)

LACE (RS)   SHEETING (RS)

• Cutting layout

Figures inside brackets show seam allowances.
Where not indicated, allow ⅜ in (1cm).

[Russel lace]
[Sheeting]

hem [1 (2.5)]
gore
hem [1 (2.5)]
hem [1 (2.5)]
skirt
hem [1 (2.5)]

2½ yd (2.3m)

45 in (110cm) wide

[Plain pink fabric]

⅔ yd (0.6m)

1⅝ (4)
waist fabric

waist measurement plus 4¾ in (12cm)

36 in (90cm) width

2. Sew left seam, insert gores

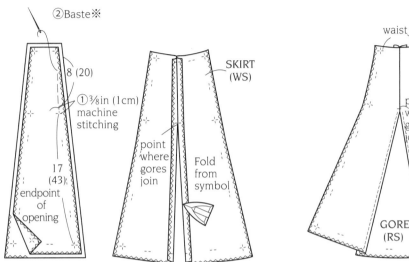

② Baste ※

8 (20)

① ⅜ in (1cm) machine stitching

17 (43)

endpoint of opening

SKIRT (WS)

point where gores join

Fold from symbol

※ Except for left side seam, stitch from point where gores join up to waist

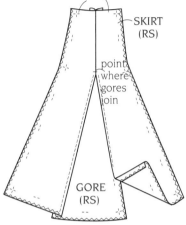

waist

SKIRT (RS)

point where gores join

GORE (RS)

Insert gores (※)

※ Apart from left side seam, topstitch in a continuous line up to waist

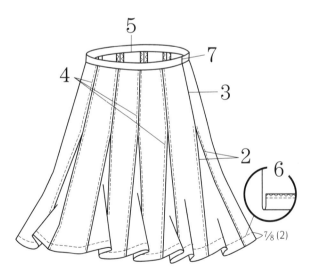

5

7

4

3

2

6

⅞ (2)

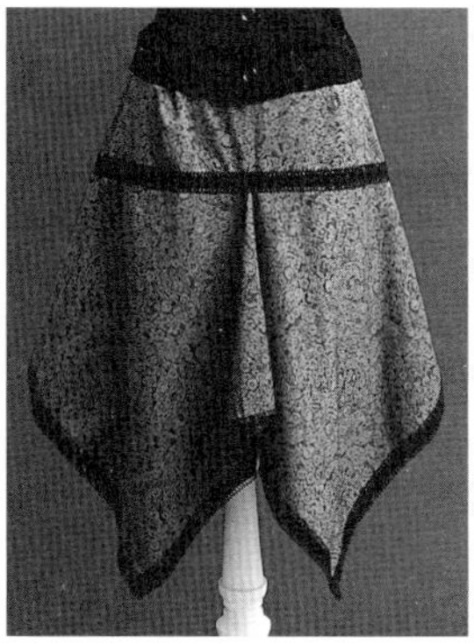

Ⓕ Skirt with Lace-trimmed Irregular Hem (photo→p.9)

MATERIALS

Fabric—Liberty Tana Lawn 44 in (110cm) wide x 1¼ yd (1.1 m)
Iron-on interfacing—⅞ in (2cm) x 7 in (18cm)
1 x invisible zipper, 9 in (22cm) long
Hook and eye
Lace—1 in (2.5cm) wide x 5 yd (4.5m)

SEWING STEPS

1. Stitch darts, sew side seams
2. Insert zipper (see p76)
3. Attach waistband (see p55)
4. Attach lace to hem
5. Attach skirt to yoke
6. Attach lace at hips over yoke and skirt seam
7. Attach hook and eye (see p63)

• Cutting layout Seam allowances are all ⅜ in (1cm)

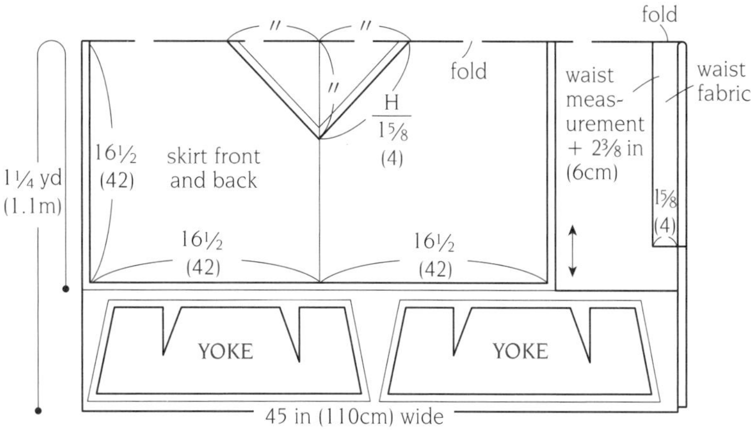

fold
fold
waist fabric
waist measurement + 2⅜ in (6cm)
H
1⅝
(4)
16½
(42)
skirt front and back
1¼ yd
(1.1m)
16½
(42)
16½
(42)
1⅝
(4)
YOKE
YOKE
45 in (110cm) wide

4.Attach lace to skirt hem

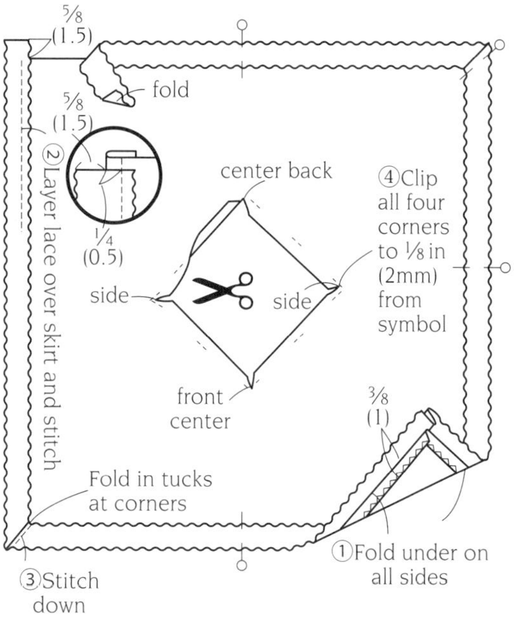

⅝
(1.5)
fold
⅝
(1.5)
②Layer lace over skirt and stitch
¼
(0.5)
center back
④Clip all four corners to ⅛ in (2mm) from symbol
side
side
front center
⅜
(1)
Fold in tucks at corners
③Stitch down
①Fold under on all sides

• Drafting (yoke)

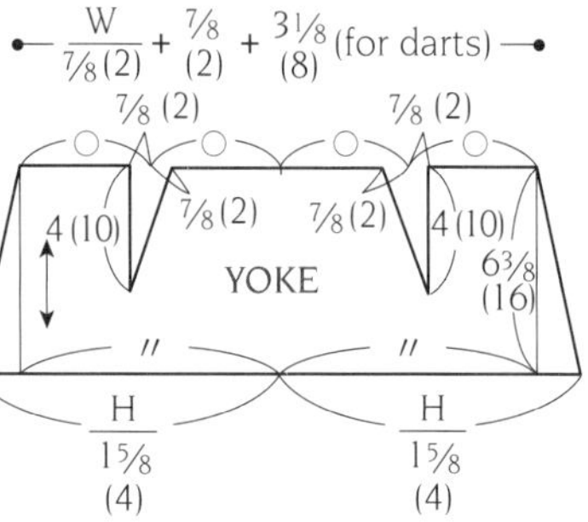

W/⅞(2) + ⅞(2) + 3⅛(8) (for darts)
⅞ (2)
⅞ (2)
⅞(2)
⅞(2)
4 (10)
4 (10)
YOKE
6⅜
(16)
H
1⅝
(4)
H
1⅝
(4)

1.Sew darts, sew sides

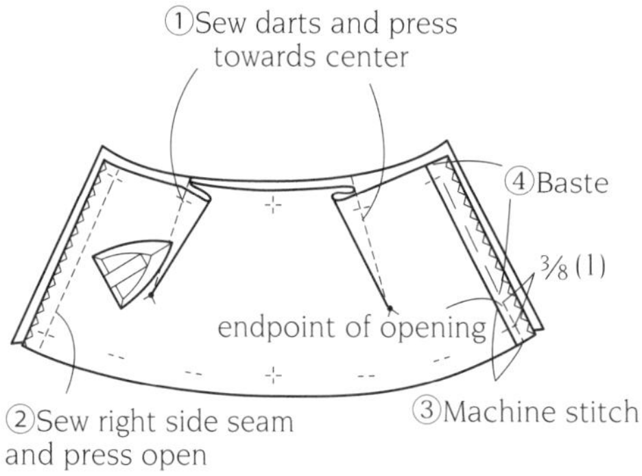

①Sew darts and press towards center
④Baste
⅜ (1)
endpoint of opening
②Sew right side seam and press open
③Machine stitch

2.Attach zipper

3.Attach waist fabric

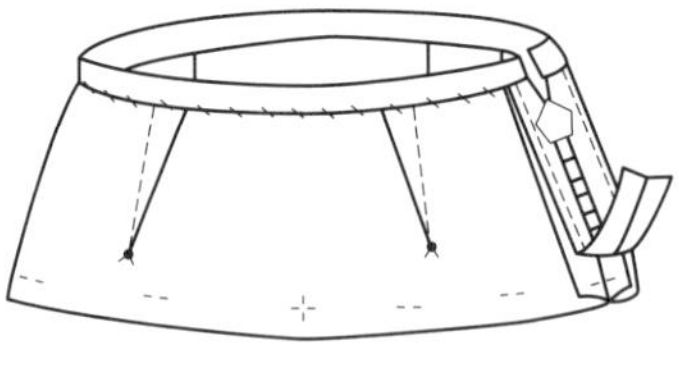

see p76, p55 for detailed instructions

5.Attach skirt to yoke

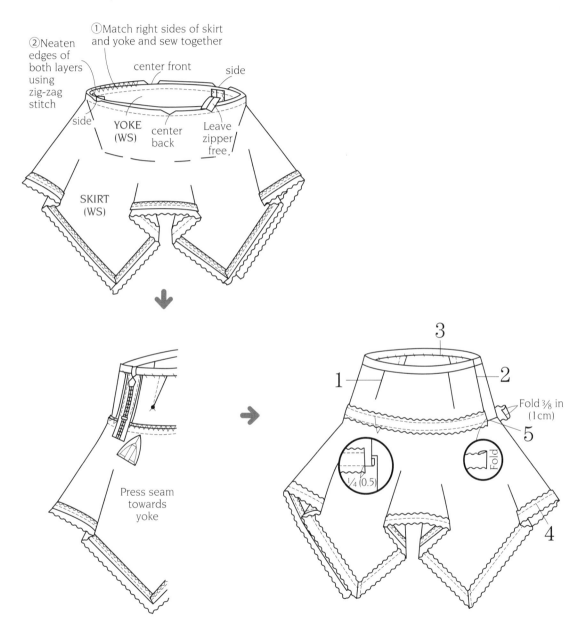

②Neaten edges of both layers using zig-zag stitch

①Match right sides of skirt and yoke and sew together

center front

side

side

YOKE (WS)

center back

Leave zipper free.

SKIRT (WS)

Press seam towards yoke

1

3

2

Fold ⅜ in (1cm)

5

¼ (0.5)

Fold

4

Ⓖ Striped Skirt with Box Pleats (photo→p.10-11)

MATERIALS

Fabric—half linen stripe 44 in (110cm) wide x 2⅛ yd (1.9m)
Lining—Bemberg 36 in (92cm) x 1½ yd (1.4m)
Iron-on interfacing—⅞ in (2cm) x 9 in (23cm)
1 x invisible zipper, 9 in (22cm) long
Hook and eye

SEWING STEPS

1. Sew skirt and inner pleat sections together to create front and back sections
2. Sew left side seam to opening and insert zipper (see p76)
3. Create hem
4. Stitch along edges of pleats
5. Topstitch pleats to endpoint of seam
6. Attach lining
7. Attach waistband
8. Attach hook and eye (see p63)

● Cutting layout (skirt)

Figures inside brackets show seam allowances.
Where not indicated, allow ⅜ in (1cm).

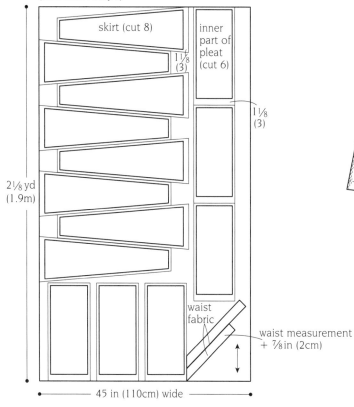

[Half linen stripe]

skirt (cut 8)

inner part of pleat (cut 6)

1⅛ (3)

1⅛ (3)

2⅛ yd (1.9m)

waist fabric

waist measurement + ⅞ in (2cm)

45 in (110cm) wide

1. Join skirt and inner part of pleats, make front and back of skirt

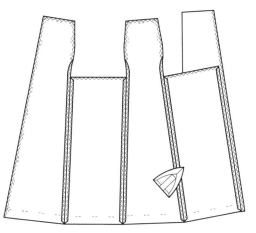

Match right sides of skirt and inner part of pleats and sew

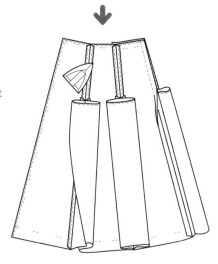

Match right sides of skirt pieces and stitch to endpoint of seam

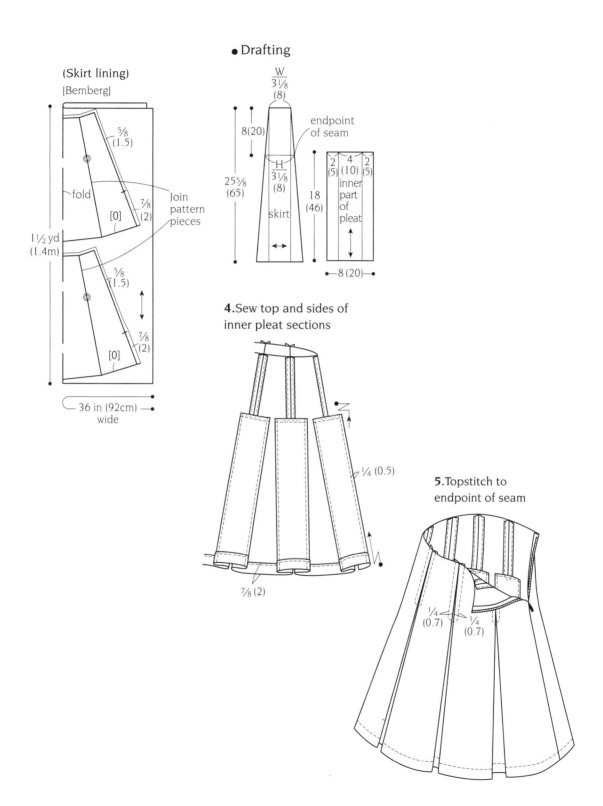

(Skirt lining)

[Bemberg]

5/8
(1.5)

fold

[0]

7/8
(2)

Join pattern pieces

5/8
(1.5)

[0]

7/8
(2)

1 1/2 yd
(1.4m)

36 in (92cm)
wide

● Drafting

W
3 1/8
(8)

8(20)

endpoint
of seam

25 5/8
(65)

H
3 1/8
(8)

skirt

18
(46)

2
(5)

4
(10)

2
(5)

inner
part
of
pleat

8 (20)

4. Sew top and sides of
inner pleat sections

1/4 (0.5)

7/8 (2)

5. Topstitch to
endpoint of seam

1/4
(0.7)

1/4
(0.7)

6.Attach lining

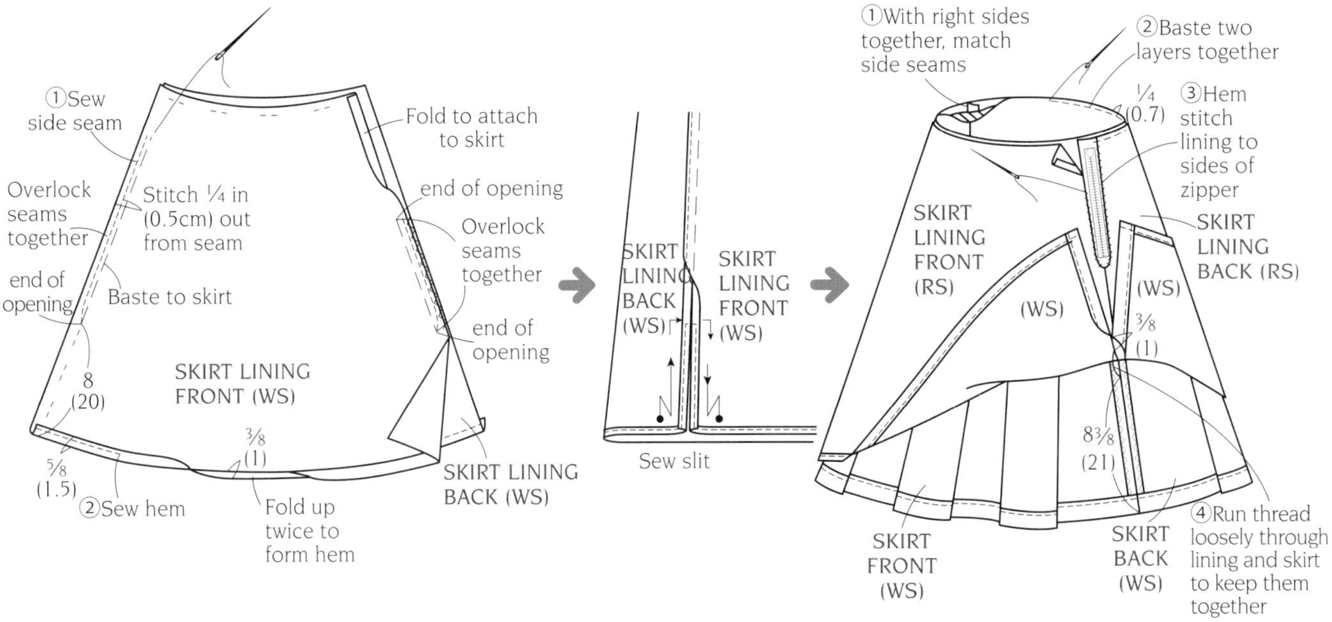
①Sew side seam
Overlock seams together
Stitch ¼ in (0.5cm) out from seam
end of opening
Baste to skirt
8 (20)
⅝ (1.5)
②Sew hem
⅜ (1)
Fold up twice to form hem
SKIRT LINING FRONT (WS)
Fold to attach to skirt
end of opening
Overlock seams together
end of opening
SKIRT LINING BACK (WS)
SKIRT LINING BACK (WS)
SKIRT LINING FRONT (WS)
Sew slit
①With right sides together, match side seams
②Baste two layers together
¼ (0.7)
③Hem stitch lining to sides of zipper
SKIRT LINING FRONT (RS)
(WS)
(WS)
SKIRT LINING BACK (RS)
⅜ (1)
8⅜ (21)
SKIRT FRONT (WS)
SKIRT BACK (WS)
④Run thread loosely through lining and skirt to keep them together

8.Attach waist binding

Match right sides of skirt (with lining attached) and waist binding and sew through all three layers

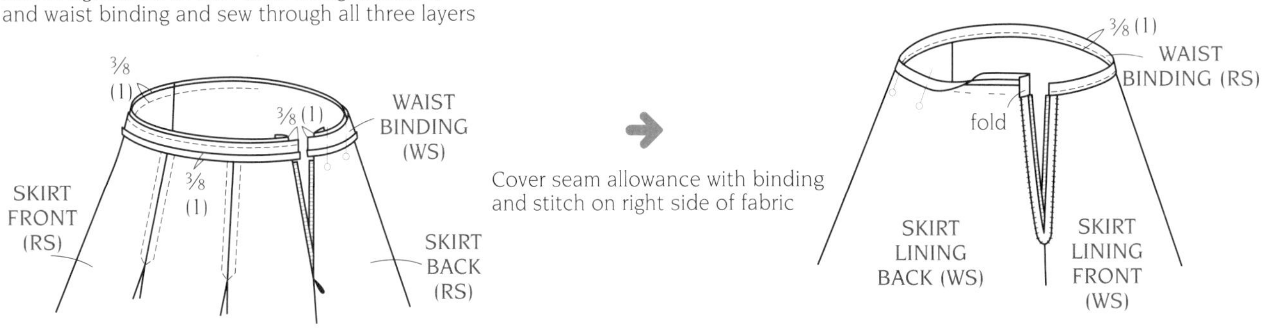
⅜ (1)
⅜ (1)
WAIST BINDING (WS)
⅜ (1)
SKIRT FRONT (RS)
SKIRT BACK (RS)
Cover seam allowance with binding and stitch on right side of fabric
⅜ (1)
WAIST BINDING (RS)
fold
SKIRT LINING BACK (WS)
SKIRT LINING FRONT (WS)

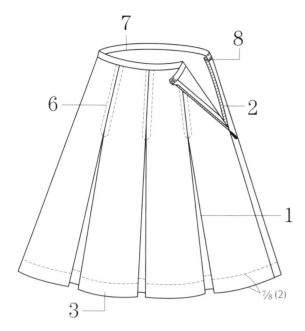

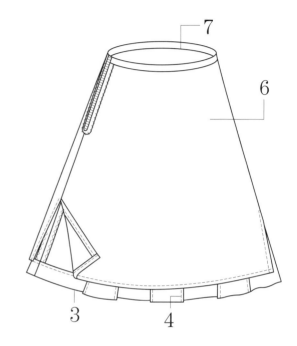

• PREPARING FABRIC

Before you start cutting, check the fabric for pulls, holes or warping that may have occurred in the weaving process. Garments created without proper fabric preparation do not hold their shape well, so this step is important. Washing fabric prior to cutting also prevents shrinkage once the garment is made up. The kind of preparation required depends on the type of fabric selected, so work out what is necessary and then test a scrap of fabric before proceeding.

• Straightening the grain of fabric

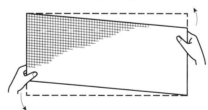

Pull fabric in direction of arrows to straighten weft threads (cotton, linen)

Put fabric into a lingerie washing bag and rinse in the washing machine or leave to soak in a basin of water for about an hour. Wring lightly and dry in shade before pressing from the reverse side, with your iron on the steam setting.

• How to iron

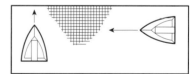

Press fabric to follow grain of warp and weft threads (silk, synthetics)

In order not to dull fabric or lose its drape, press using a dry iron on the reverse side of fabric. Press with a cloth over fabric if necessary.

🄷 Tiered-look Frill Skirt (photo→p.12)

MATERIALS

Fabric—durable, washable lawn chintz (for skirt)
   44 in (110cm) x 1¼ yd (1.1 m)
Sweatshirt mesh (for frill) 45 in (115cm) x 1⅓ yd (1.2m)
Belt elastic—1 in (2.5cm) wide x [your waist measurement
   x 0.9 +⅞ in (2cm)]
Embroidery thread—blue

SEWING STEPS

1. Sew the frill
2. Make side seams of upper skirt and lower skirt
3. Sew waist casing
4. Attach frills to skirt
5. Join upper and lower skirt sections
6. Insert elastic into waist casing

1.Sew frills

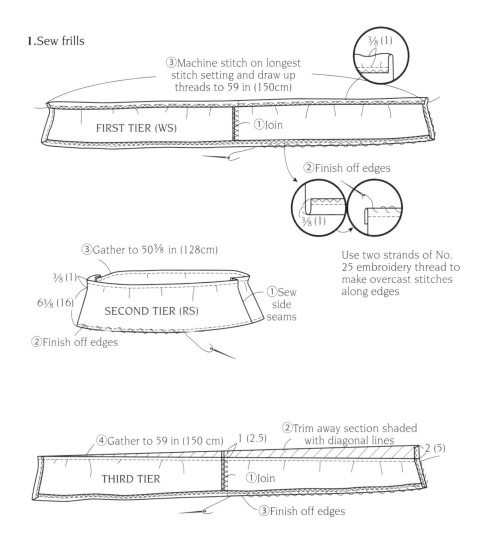

③Machine stitch on longest stitch setting and draw up threads to 59 in (150cm)

⅜ (1)

FIRST TIER (WS)

①Join

②Finish off edges

⅜ (1)

Use two strands of No. 25 embroidery thread to make overcast stitches along edges

③Gather to 50⅜ in (128cm)

⅜ (1)

6⅜ (16)

SECOND TIER (RS)

①Sew side seams

②Finish off edges

④Gather to 59 in (150 cm)

1 (2.5)

②Trim away section shaded with diagonal lines

2 (5)

THIRD TIER

①Join

③Finish off edges

4.Attach frills to skirt

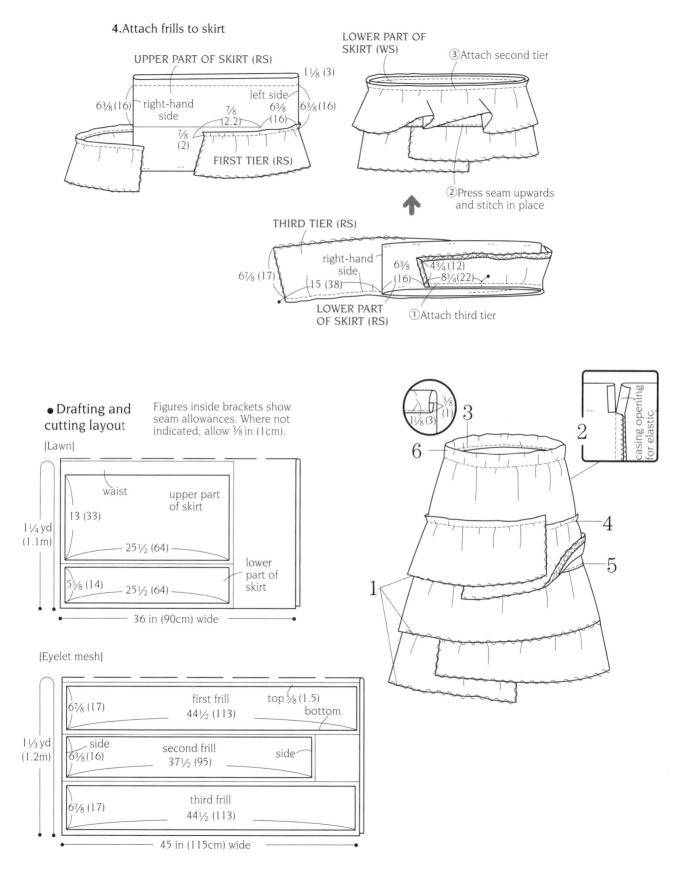

UPPER PART OF SKIRT (RS)

1⅛ (3)

6⅜(16) right-hand side

left side

⅞ (2.2)

6⅜ (16)

6⅜ (16)

⅞ (2)

FIRST TIER (RS)

LOWER PART OF SKIRT (WS)

③Attach second tier

②Press seam upwards and stitch in place

THIRD TIER (RS)

right-hand side

6⅞ (17)

15 (38)

6⅜ (16)

4¾ (12)

8¾ (22)

LOWER PART OF SKIRT (RS)

①Attach third tier

● **Drafting and cutting layout**

Figures inside brackets show seam allowances. Where not indicated, allow ⅜ in (1cm).

[Lawn]

1¼ yd (1.1m)

waist

upper part of skirt

13 (33)

25½ (64)

lower part of skirt

5⅝ (14)

25½ (64)

36 in (90cm) wide

[Eyelet mesh]

1⅓ yd (1.2m)

6⅞ (17)

first frill
44½ (113)

top ⅝ (1.5)

bottom

side

6⅜(16)

second frill
37½ (95)

side

6⅞ (17)

third frill
44½ (113)

45 in (115cm) wide

⅜ (1)

1⅛ (3)

3

6

2

casing opening for elastic

4

5

1

❶ Long Jacquard "Escargot" Skirt with Straight Hem Panel (photo→p.13)

MATERIAL

Fabric—jacquard 56 in (142cm) wide x $1\frac{7}{8}$ yd (1.7m)※
Iron-on interfacing—$\frac{7}{8}$ in (2cm) x $8\frac{1}{4}$ in (21cm)
1 x invisible zipper, 9 in (22cm) long
Hook and eye
※ For hips measuring up to $37\frac{3}{4}$ in (96cm), $1\frac{7}{8}$ yd (1.7m) is required. For hips over $37\frac{3}{4}$ in (96cm), multiply the hem width by five and add $\frac{7}{8}$ in (2cm) to calculate the required fabric length.

SEWING STEPS

1. Join all five panels together
2. Sew left side to opening and attach zipper (see p76)
3. Open out seams of left side and stitch on both sides of seam
4. Attach waistband
5. Create hem and attach hem panel
6. Attach hook and eye (see p63)

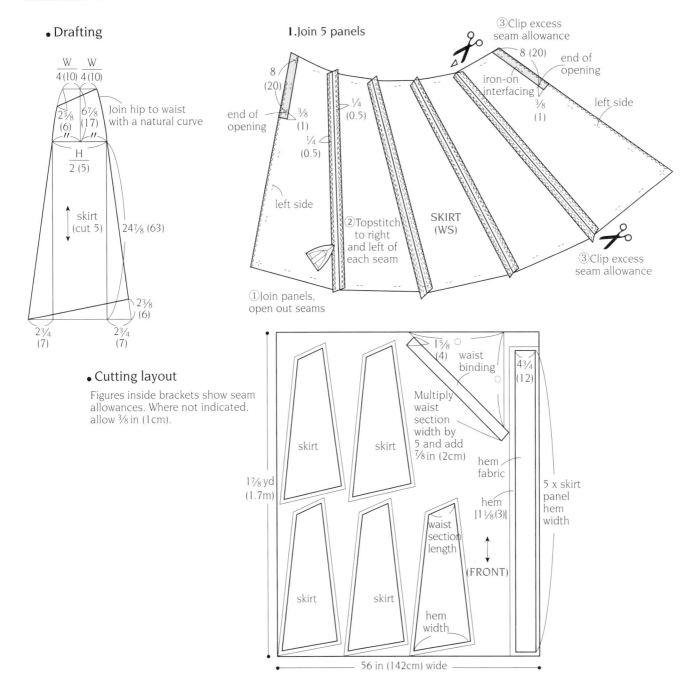

- Drafting

$\frac{W}{4}$ (10) $\frac{W}{4}$ (10)

Join hip to waist with a natural curve

$2\frac{3}{8}$ (6) $6\frac{7}{8}$ (17)

$\frac{H}{2}$ (5)

skirt (cut 5) $24\frac{7}{8}$ (63)

$2\frac{3}{8}$ (6)

$2\frac{3}{4}$ (7) $2\frac{3}{4}$ (7)

- Cutting layout

Figures inside brackets show seam allowances. Where not indicated, allow $\frac{3}{8}$ in (1cm).

1.Join 5 panels

③Clip excess seam allowance

8 (20)

end of opening

iron-on interfacing

left side

8 (20)

end of opening

$\frac{3}{8}$ (1)

$\frac{1}{4}$ (0.5)

$\frac{3}{8}$ (1)

$\frac{1}{4}$ (0.5)

left side

②Topstitch to right and left of each seam

SKIRT (WS)

③Clip excess seam allowance

①Join panels, open out seams

$1\frac{5}{8}$ (4)   waist binding

$4\frac{3}{4}$ (12)

Multiply waist section width by 5 and add $\frac{7}{8}$ in (2cm)

hem fabric

hem [$1\frac{1}{8}$ (3)]

5 x skirt panel hem width

skirt   skirt

$1\frac{7}{8}$ yd (1.7m)

waist section length

(FRONT)

skirt   skirt

hem width

56 in (142cm) wide

4.Attach waist binding

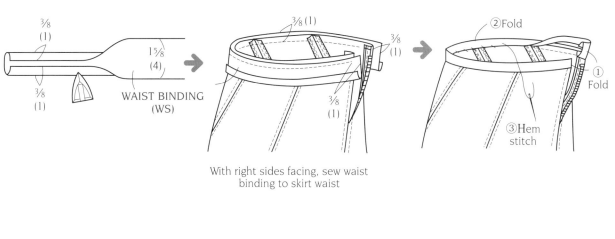

¾
(1)

¾
(1)

1⅝
(4)

WAIST BINDING
(WS)

¾ (1)

¾
(1)

¾
(1)

With right sides facing, sew waist
binding to skirt waist

②Fold

①
Fold

③Hem
stitch

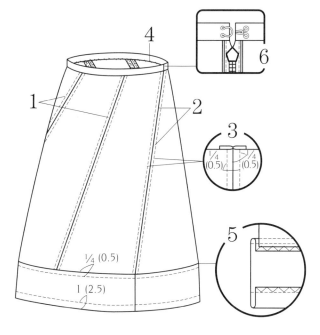

4

1

2

6

3

¼
(0.5)

¼
(0.5)

5

¼ (0.5)

1 (2.5)

❹ Skirt with Irregular Gathering (photo→p.14-15)

MATERIALS

Fabric—cotton lace 41 in (102cm) x 2⅓ yd (2.1 m)
Iron-on interfacing—⅞ in (2cm) x 2¾ in (7cm)
Elastic—⅜ in (0.8cm) wide x [your waist measurement
    x 0.9 + ⅞ in (2cm)]—two pieces

SEWING STEPS

1. Join skirt sections
2. Attach waist casing
3. Create drawstring
4. Insert elastic and drawstring into waist
    casing
5. Create hem

• Cutting layout

Figures inside brackets show seam allowances.
Where not indicated, allow ⅜in (1cm).

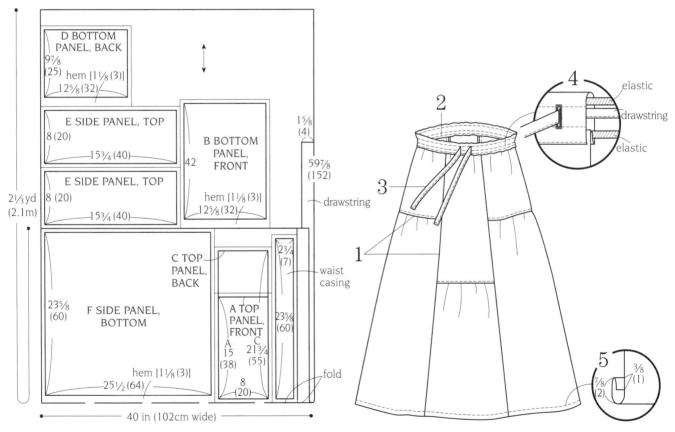

1. Join panels

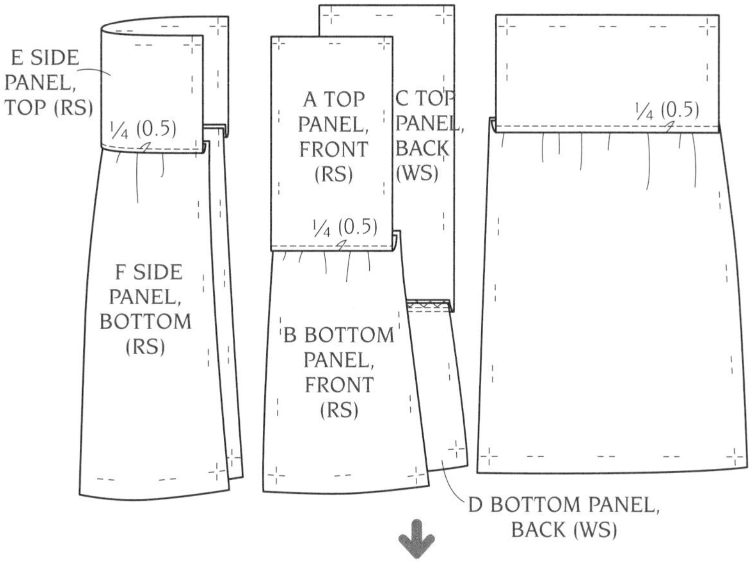
E SIDE PANEL, TOP (RS)
¼ (0.5)
F SIDE PANEL, BOTTOM (RS)
A TOP PANEL, FRONT (RS)
C TOP PANEL, BACK (WS)
¼ (0.5)
B BOTTOM PANEL, FRONT (RS)
D BOTTOM PANEL, BACK (WS)
¼ (0.5)

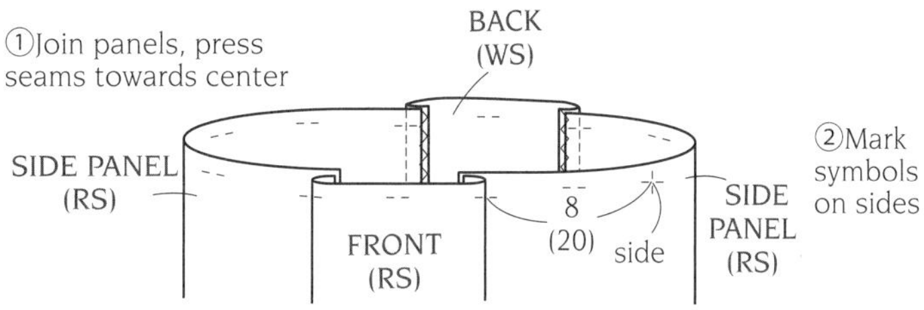
①Join panels, press seams towards center
BACK (WS)
SIDE PANEL (RS)
FRONT (RS)
8 (20)
side
SIDE PANEL (RS)
②Mark symbols on sides

2. Attach waist casing

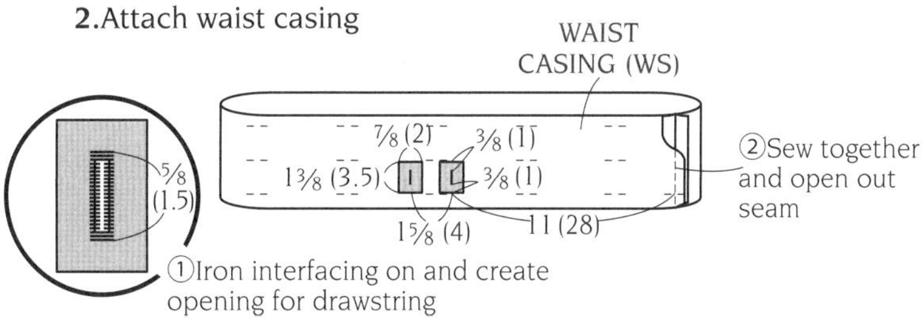
WAIST CASING (WS)
⅝ (1.5)
⅞ (2)
⅜ (1)
1⅜ (3.5)
⅜ (1)
1⅝ (4)
11 (28)
②Sew together and open out seam
①Iron interfacing on and create opening for drawstring

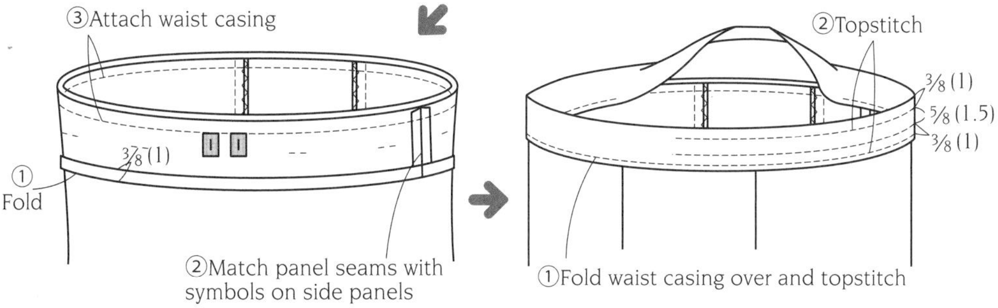
③Attach waist casing
⅜ (1)
① Fold
②Match panel seams with symbols on side panels
②Topstitch
⅜ (1)
⅝ (1.5)
⅜ (1)
①Fold waist casing over and topstitch

3. Create drawstring

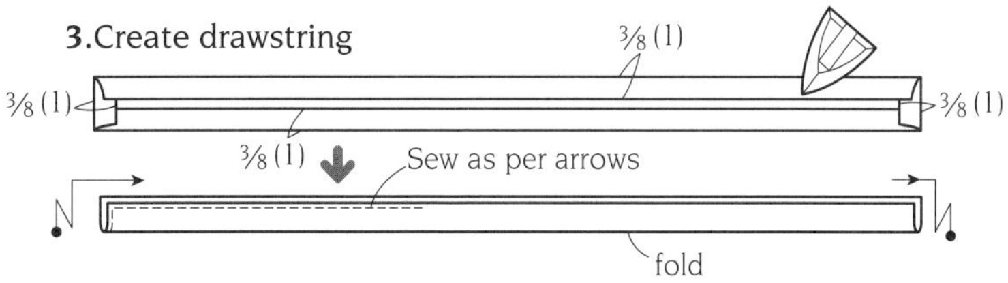
⅜ (1)
⅜ (1)
⅜ (1)
⅜ (1)
Sew as per arrows
fold

ⓚ Wrap Skirt with Frilled Edge (photo→p.16)

MATERIALS
Fabric—44 in (112cm) wide x 1⅔ yd (1.5m)

SEWING STEPS
1. Create frill
2. Attach frill to skirt
3. Create waist tie
4. Complete waist section

● Cutting layout

Figures inside brackets show seam allowances.
Where not indicated, allow ⅜ in (1cm).

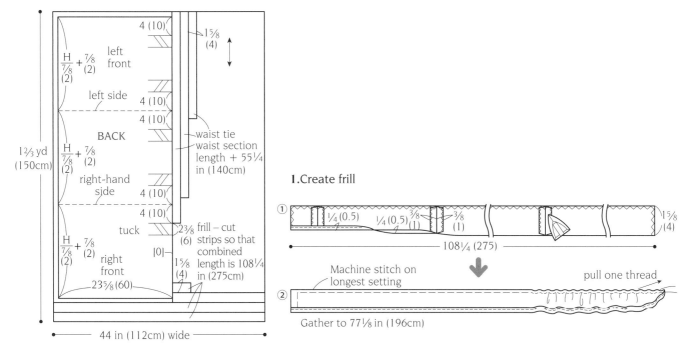

1.Create frill

Machine stitch on longest setting

pull one thread

Gather to 77⅛ in (196cm)

2.Attach frill

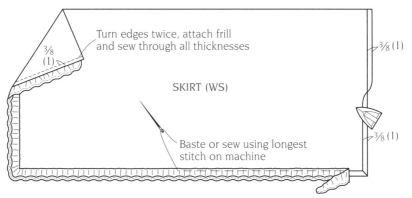

Turn edges twice, attach frill and sew through all thicknesses

⅜ (1)

SKIRT (WS)

⅜ (1)

⅜ (1)

Baste or sew using longest stitch on machine

3. Create waist tie

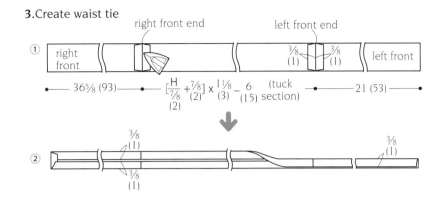

① right front   right front end   left front end   ³⁄₈ (1) ³⁄₈ (1)   left front

$$\bullet\!-\!36\tfrac{5}{8}\,(93)\!-\!\bullet\quad [\tfrac{H}{7\tfrac{7}{8}\,(2)}+\tfrac{7}{8}\,(2)]\times\tfrac{1\tfrac{1}{8}}{(3)}-\tfrac{6}{(15)}\ \text{(tuck section)}\quad\bullet\!-\!21\,(53)\!-\!\bullet$$

②   ³⁄₈ (1)   ³⁄₈ (1)   ³⁄₈ (1)

4. Finish off waist

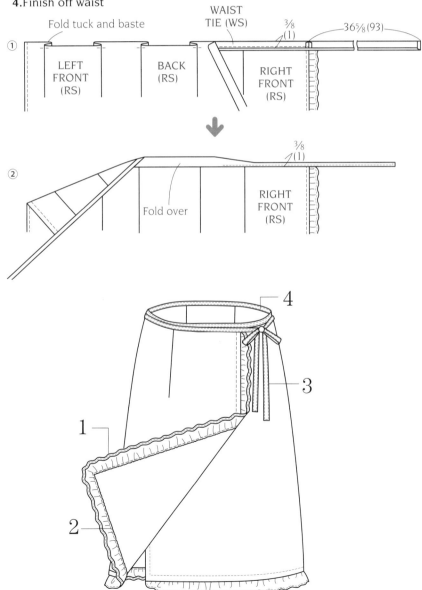

① Fold tuck and baste   WAIST TIE (WS)   ³⁄₈ (1)   36⅝ (93)

LEFT FRONT (RS)   BACK (RS)   RIGHT FRONT (RS)

② ³⁄₈ (1)   Fold over   RIGHT FRONT (RS)

4

3

1

2

● Trapezoid Skirt with Line Detail (photo→p.17)

MATERIALS

Fabric—52 in (130cm) wide x 3⅓ yd (3m)
Iron-on interfacing—2⅜ in (6cm) x 31½ in (80cm)
1 x invisible zipper, 9 in (22cm) long
Hook and eye
Grosgrain tape—¼ in (0.6cm) wide x 3⅓ yd (3m)

SEWING STEPS

1. Join five panels together for skirt front and grosgrain tape. Repeat for skirt back
2. Sew left side to opening and attach zipper (see p76)
3. Sew right side and create hem
4. Stitch along pleats on inside and outside of skirt
5. Attach waistband (see p50)
6. Attach hook and eye (see p63)

● Drafting

● Cutting layout

Cut fabric as per measurements in diagram

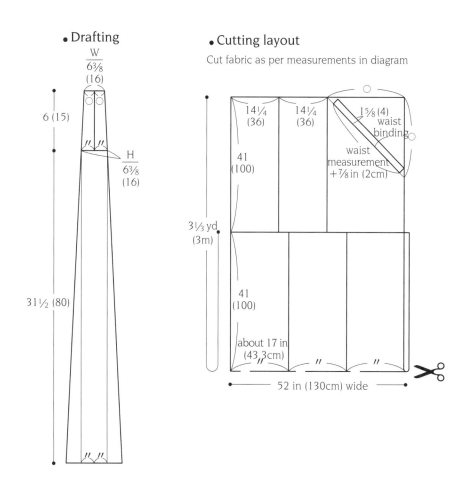

Use two pieces of fabric.
Fold each vertically with
right sides together

6 pieces

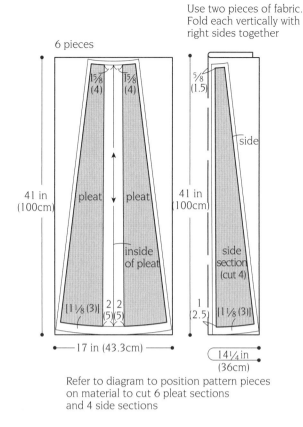

1⁵⁄₈ (4)   1⁵⁄₈ (4)

⁵⁄₈ (1.5)

side

pleat   pleat

41 in (100cm)

41 in (100cm)

inside of pleat

side section (cut 4)

[1¹⁄₈ (3)]   2 (5) 2 (5)

1 (2.5)   [1¹⁄₈ (3)]

17 in (43.3cm)

14¹⁄₄ in (36cm)

Refer to diagram to position pattern pieces
on material to cut 6 pleat sections
and 4 side sections

1.Join 5 panels each for front and back and attach grosgrain tape

① Join 3 pleat sections each
for front and back
② Attach side sections at left
and right for both front and back
③ Stitch both edges of grosgrain tape
④ Iron on interfacing where zipper
will be attached

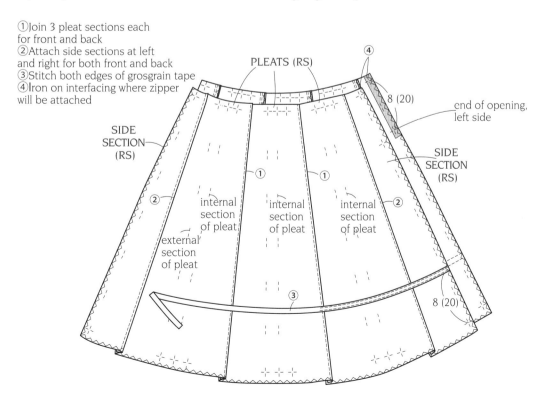

PLEATS (RS)

④

8 (20)

end of opening,
left side

SIDE SECTION (RS)

SIDE SECTION (RS)

②   ②

①   ①

internal section of pleat   internal section of pleat   internal section of pleat

external section of pleat

③

8 (20)

4. Stitch edges of pleats, inner and outer

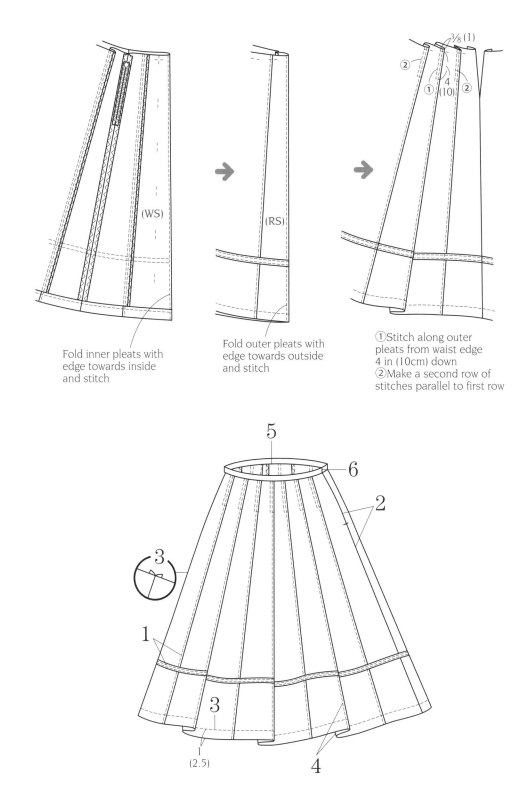

Fold inner pleats with edge towards inside and stitch

Fold outer pleats with edge towards outside and stitch

③⁄₈ (1)

④
(10)

①Stitch along outer pleats from waist edge 4 in (10cm) down
②Make a second row of stitches parallel to first row

5

6

2

3

1

3

1
(2.5)

4

● Attaching skirt hook and bar

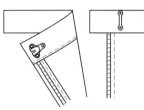

 ①Knot thread and backstitch fabric at hook position

 ②Insert needle through hook hole from flat side and back through hole under flat side

 ③Bring needle through thread loop

 ④Pull thread firmly

 ⑤Repeat steps②~④ several times, working counter-clockwise

 ⑥At the top of the hook, bring needle around flat side and through next hole

 ⑦Pass needle through last few stitches and knot to finish

 ⑧Bring needle under hook and clip thread

● Attaching hook and eye

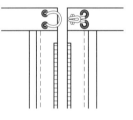 Stitch as shown

Pass needle over hook and through fabric

Make 2-3 stitches

● How to attach buttons

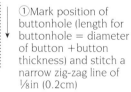 ①Use thread to create shank as long as the width of the fabric through which button will pass

 ②Repeat 2-3 times

③Wind thread around shank firmly and pull tight

④Knot on underside of fabric. Bring needle back to right side and clip thread

● Creating buttonholes

①Mark position of buttonhole (length for buttonhole = diameter of button +button thickness) and stitch a narrow zig-zag line of ⅛in (0.2cm)

②Stitch at position "0" 5 times using ³⁄₁₆in (0.4cm) wide stitch

③Make another line of stitching in the same way as ①

 ④Finish off the buttonhole by repeating ②

⑤Use seam ripper to slash between the rows of stitching. Insert a pin at the top of the buttonhole first to prevent it being slashed

Ⓜ Denim Skirt with Patch Pocket (photo→p.18)

MATERIALS
Fabric—8-ounce denim 58 in (145cm) wide x 1⅓ yd (1.2m)
Iron-on interfacing—20 in (50cm) x 12 in (30cm)
1 x invisible zipper, 9 in (22cm) long
Hook and eye

SEWING STEPS
1. Sew darts
2. Sew panels for right front section
3. Sew center back
4. Attach pockets
5. Sew left side to opening and insert zipper (see p76)
6. Sew right side
7. Attach facing
8. Create hem
9. Attach hook and eye (see p63)

• Drafting

• Cutting layout

Figures inside brackets show seam allowances.
Where not indicated, allow ⅜ in (1cm).

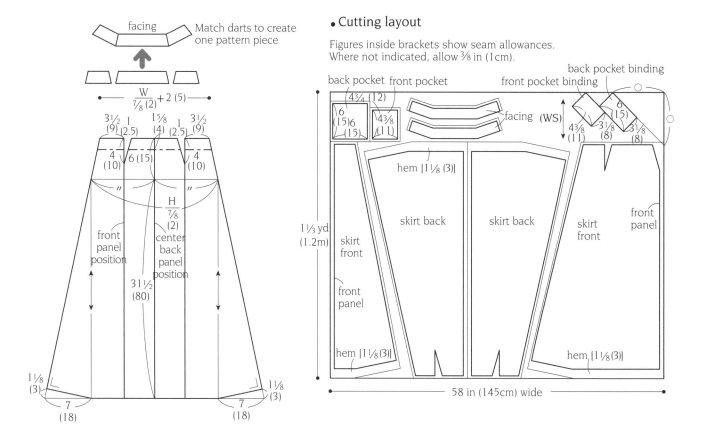

1. Sew darts

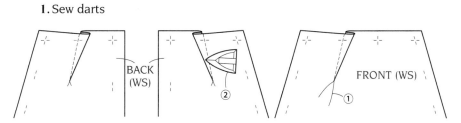

① Sew darts, knot end of thread and clip excess thread
② Press dart towards center

4. Attach pockets

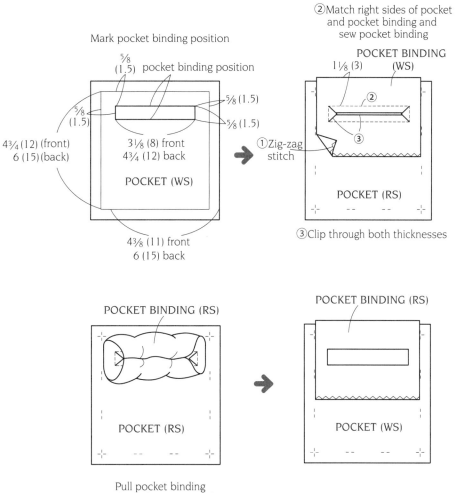

② Match right sides of pocket and pocket binding and sew pocket binding

Mark pocket binding position

⅝ (1.5) pocket binding position

⅝ (1.5)
⅝ (1.5)
⅝ (1.5)

POCKET BINDING (WS)

1⅛ (3)

① Zig-zag stitch

③ Clip through both thicknesses

4¾ (12) (front)
6 (15)(back)

3⅛ (8) front
4¾ (12) back

POCKET (WS)

POCKET (RS)

4⅜ (11) front
6 (15) back

POCKET BINDING (RS)

POCKET (RS)

Pull pocket binding through to wrong side

POCKET BINDING (RS)

POCKET (WS)

4. Attach pockets (continued)

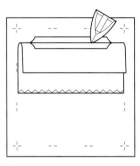

Open out seams
(repeat for underside)

POCKET BINDING (RS)

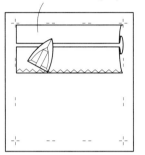

Fold binding as per diagram
and press

POCKET (RS)

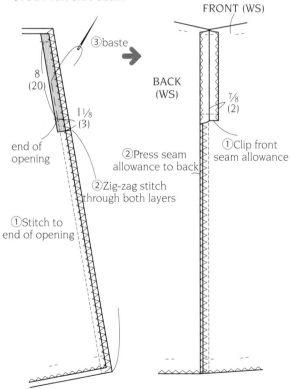

Stitch

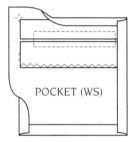

POCKET (WS)

Fold edges from symbols

pocket opening

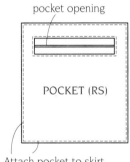

POCKET (RS)

Attach pocket to skirt
at marked position

5. Sew left side seam

FRONT (WS)

③baste

8
(20)

1⅛
(3)

end of
opening

①Stitch to
end of opening

②Zig-zag stitch
through both layers

BACK
(WS)

②Press seam
allowance to back

⅞
(2)

①Clip front
seam allowance

7. Attach facing

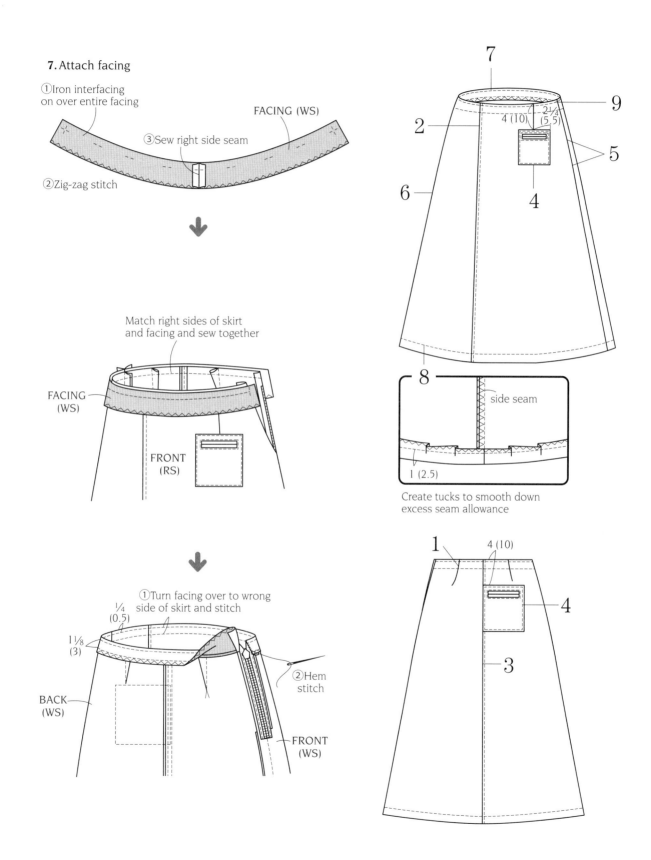

① Iron interfacing on over entire facing

FACING (WS)

③ Sew right side seam

② Zig-zag stitch

Match right sides of skirt and facing and sew together

FACING (WS)

FRONT (RS)

① Turn facing over to wrong side of skirt and stitch

¼ (0.5)

1⅛ (3)

BACK (WS)

② Hem stitch

FRONT (WS)

7

2

9

2¼ (5.5)

4 (10)

5

6

4

8

side seam

1 (2.5)

Create tucks to smooth down excess seam allowance

1

4 (10)

4

3

❶ Tucked and Gathered Cotton Skirt (photo→p.19)

MATERIALS
Fabric—slub cotton 44 (106cm) wide x 1⅔ yd (1.5m)
Iron-on interfacing—⅞ in (2cm) x 9 in (23cm)
1 x invisible zipper, 9 in (22cm) long
Hook and eye
Lattice lace ribbon—1⅛ in (3cm) wide x [your waist measurement + 53½ in (136cm)]
Grosgrain tape— ⅜ in (1cm) wide x [your waist measurement + 53½ in (136cm)]

SEWING STEPS
1. Attach lace to skirt
2. Sew left side to opening and insert zipper (see p76)
3. Create hem
4. Baste tucks
5. Attach waistband (see p50)
6. Attach hook and eye (see p63)

● Cutting layout

Figures inside brackets show seam allowances.
Where not indicated, allow ⅜ in (1cm).

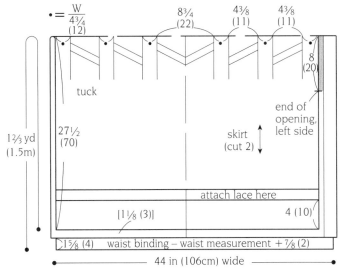

$\bullet = \dfrac{W}{4\frac{3}{4}}$ (12)

8¾ (22) 4⅜ (11) 4⅜ (11)

8 (20)

tuck

end of opening, left side

27½ (70)

1⅔ yd (1.5m)

skirt (cut 2)

attach lace here

[1⅛ (3)]   4 (10)

1⅝ (4)   waist binding – waist measurement + ⅞ (2)

44 in (106cm) wide

● How to fold tucks

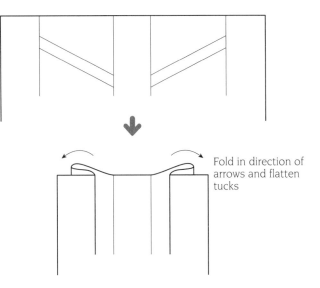

Fold in direction of arrows and flatten tucks

1. Attach lattice lace

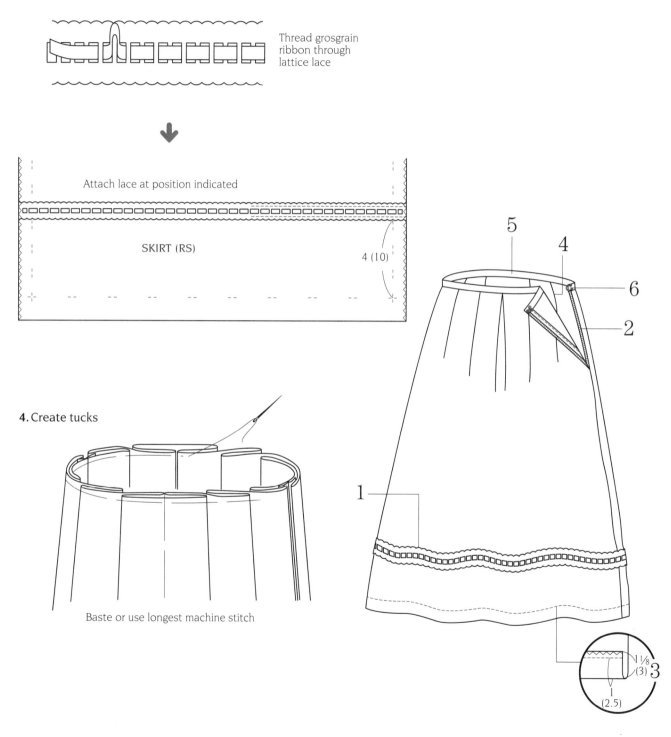

Thread grosgrain ribbon through lattice lace

Attach lace at position indicated

SKIRT (RS)

4 (10)

4. Create tucks

Baste or use longest machine stitch

5

4

6

2

1

1⅛
(3)

3

1
(2.5)

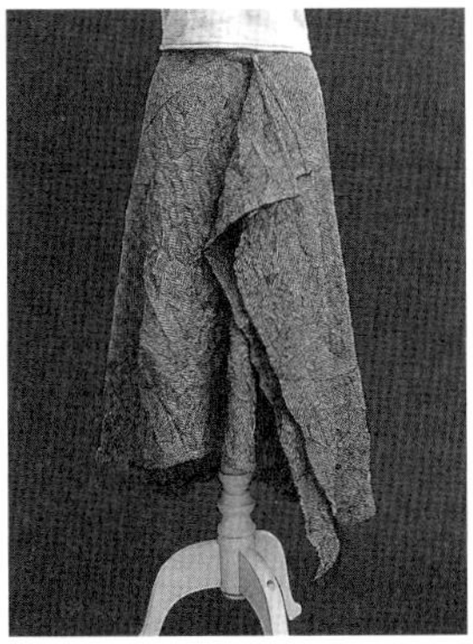

⓿ Tweed Skirt with Panel Detail (photo→p.20-21)

MATERIALS

Fabric—washable Tweed 52 in (130cm) wide x 1¾ yd (1.6m)
Iron-on interfacing—⅞ in (2cm) x 9 in (23cm)
1 x invisible zipper, 9 in (22cm) long
Hook and eye

SEWING STEPS

1. Join all parts from the right front panel to the back of the skirt
2. Sew left side until opening and insert zipper (see p76)
3. Create hem
4. Match front right and front left panels and stitch together
5. Create waist
6. Attach hook and eye (see p63)

1. Starting with front right panel and working towards the back of the skirt, sew all parts of skirt together

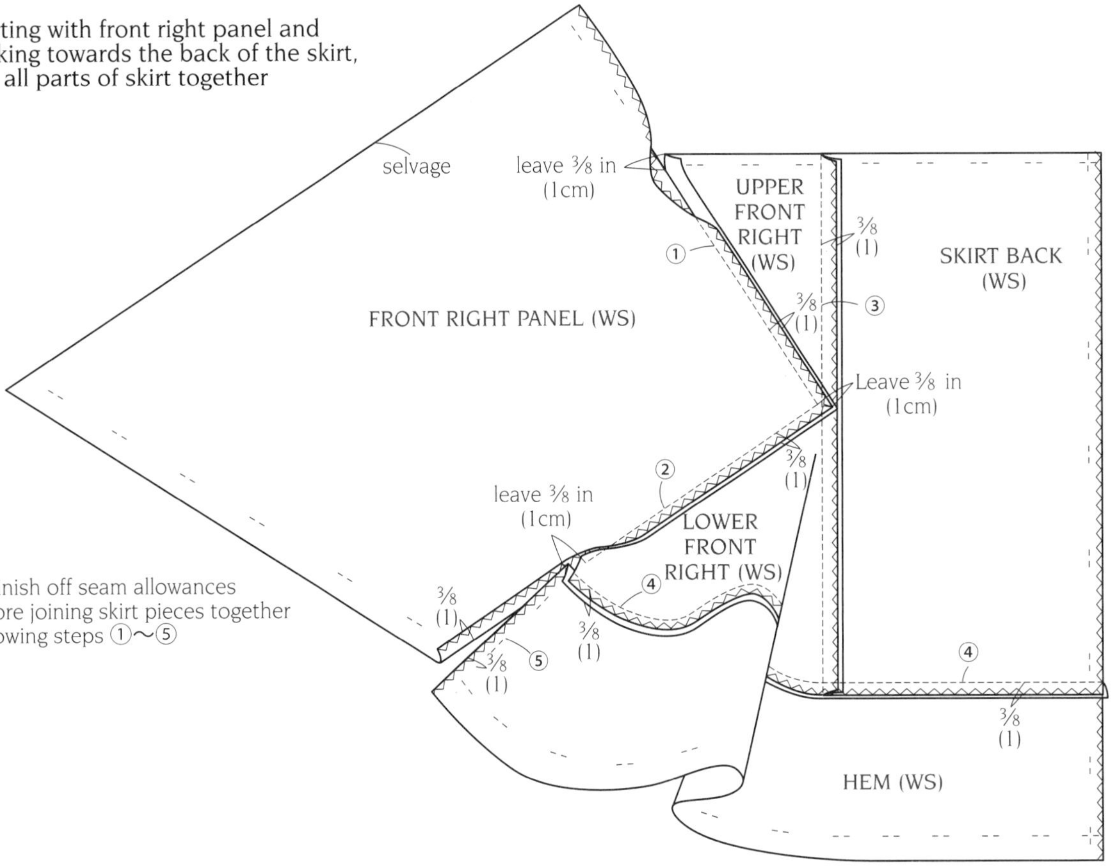
selvage
leave ⅜ in (1cm)
UPPER FRONT RIGHT (WS)
⅜ (1)
SKIRT BACK (WS)
①
⅜ (1)
③
FRONT RIGHT PANEL (WS)
Leave ⅜ in (1cm)
②
⅜ (1)
leave ⅜ in (1cm)
LOWER FRONT RIGHT (WS)
④
⅜ (1)
⅜ (1)
⑤
⅜ (1)
④
⅜ (1)
HEM (WS)

※Finish off seam allowances before joining skirt pieces together following steps ①~⑤

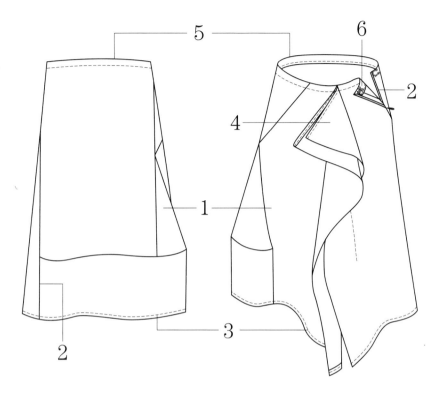

3. Finish off hem

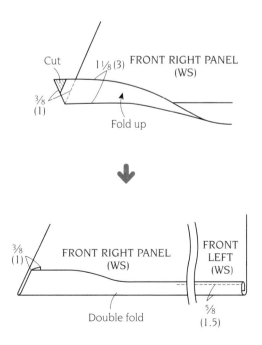

4. Match front right and front left panels and sew

Match right sides of front right and front left panels at ☆ symbol and sew

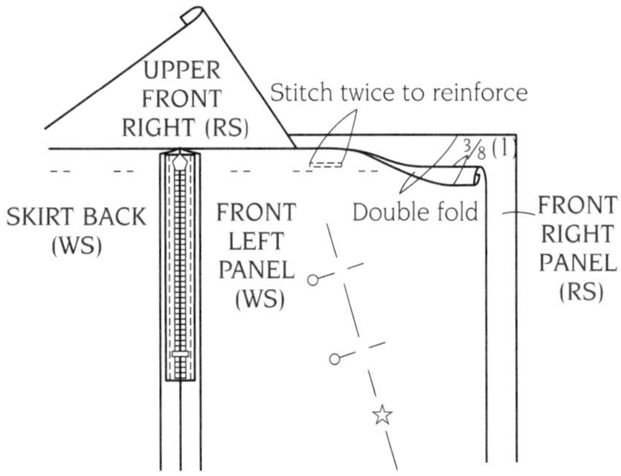
UPPER FRONT RIGHT (RS)
Stitch twice to reinforce
3/8 (1)
SKIRT BACK (WS)
FRONT LEFT PANEL (WS)
Double fold
FRONT RIGHT PANEL (RS)
☆

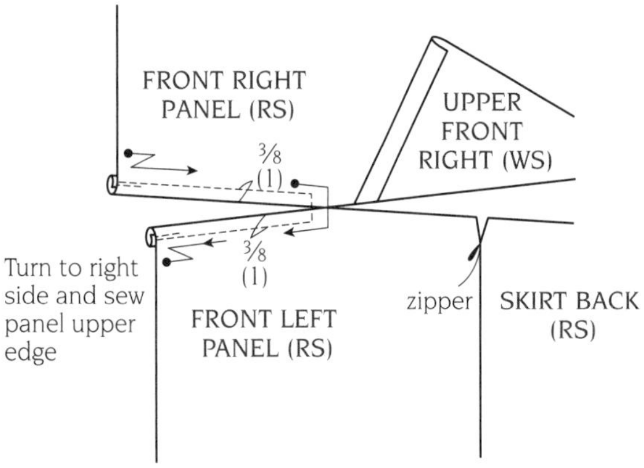
FRONT RIGHT PANEL (RS)
3/8 (1)
UPPER FRONT RIGHT (WS)
3/8 (1)
Turn to right side and sew panel upper edge
FRONT LEFT PANEL (RS)
zipper
SKIRT BACK (RS)

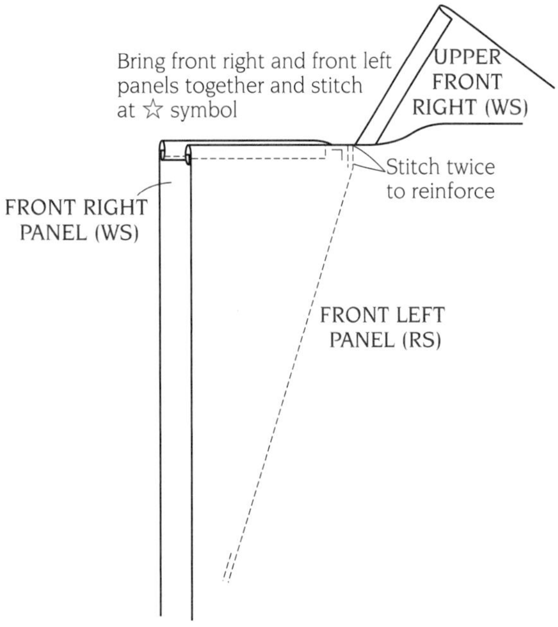
Bring front right and front left panels together and stitch at ☆ symbol
UPPER FRONT RIGHT (WS)
Stitch twice to reinforce
FRONT RIGHT PANEL (WS)
FRONT LEFT PANEL (RS)

5. Finish off waist

Match right sides of skirt and facing and sew together

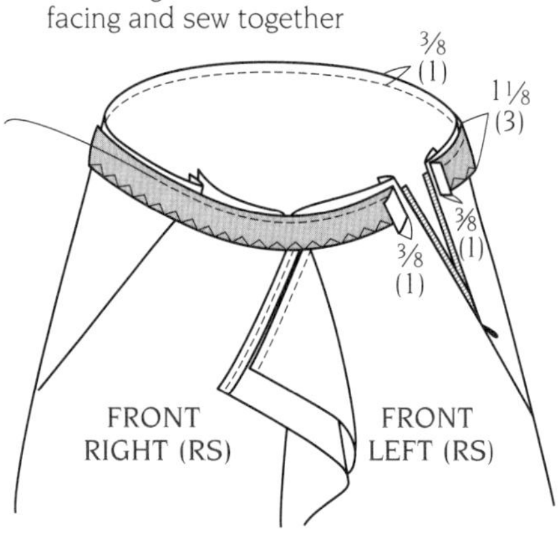
3/8 (1)
1 1/8 (3)
3/8 (1)
3/8 (1)
FRONT RIGHT (RS)
FRONT LEFT (RS)

Turn to wrong side and stitch down on either side of panels

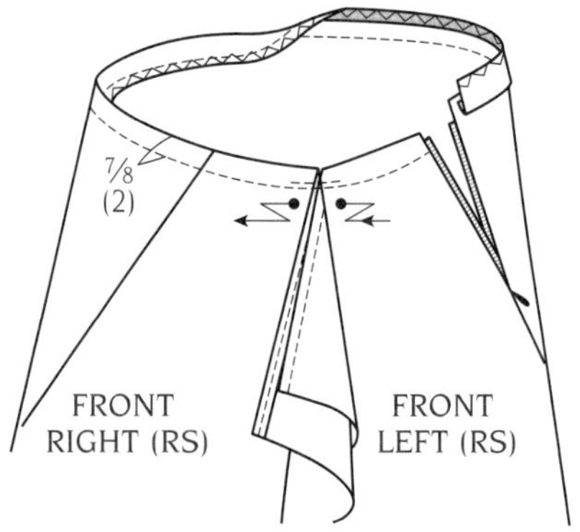
7/8 (2)
FRONT RIGHT (RS)
FRONT LEFT (RS)

● Drafting

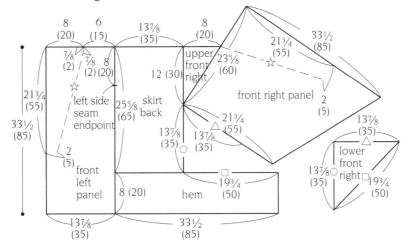

● Cutting layout

Figures inside brackets show seam allowances.
Where not indicated, allow ⅜ in (1cm).

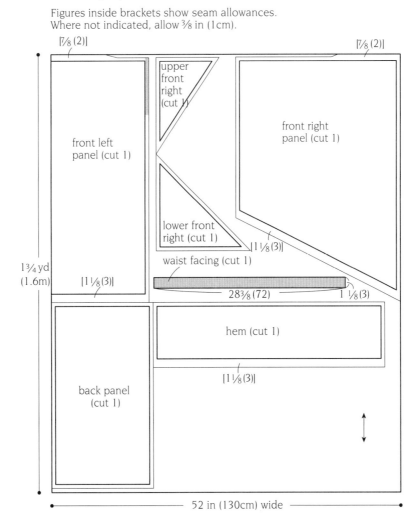

P **Long Balloon Skirt** (photo→p.22)
Q **Black Balloon Skirt** (photo→p.23)

MATERIALS

Fabric—Crushed satin 50 in (122cm) wide x 2½ yd (2.2m)
[P]/1⅔ yd (1.5m) [Q]
Lining—Bemberg 36 in (92cm) wide x 1⅞ yd (1.7m)
[P]/1⅓ yd (1.2m) [Q]
Iron-on interfacing—each 2⅜ in (6cm) x 32 in (78cm)
1 x invisible zipper, 9 in (22cm) long, for each skirt

SEWING STEPS

1. Make marks for tucks and baste tucks
2. Sew side seams of outer skirt section and attach zipper
3. Sew side seams of lining
4. Sew outer and inner skirt sections together
5. Attach waistband casing
6. Create cord and insert into waist casing

1. Fold tucks

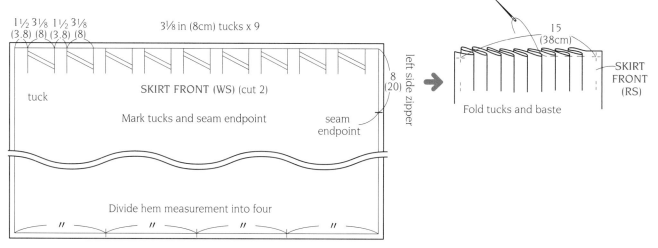

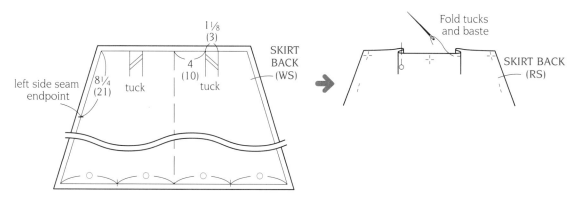

symbols for four hem sections

● Drafting and cutting layout (skirt)

Figures inside brackets show seam allowances.
Where not indicated, allow ⅜ in (1cm).

[Crushed satin]

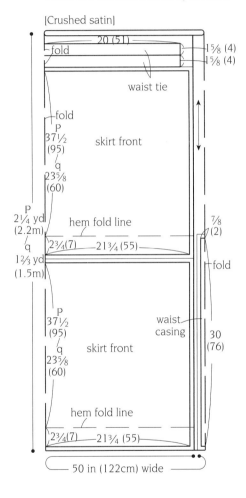

(Skirt lining)
[Bemberg]

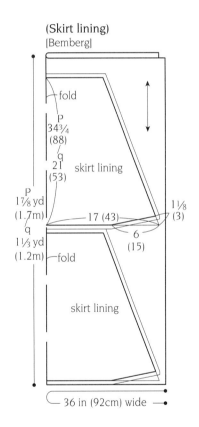

2. Sew side seams of skirt, attach zipper

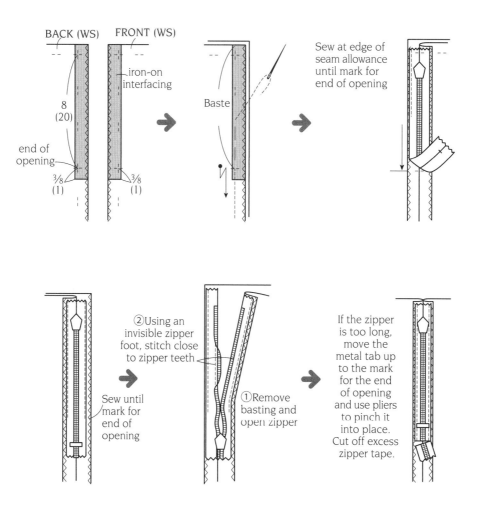

BACK (WS)   FRONT (WS)

iron-on interfacing

8 (20)

end of opening

3/8 (1)   3/8 (1)

Baste

Sew at edge of seam allowance until mark for end of opening

② Using an invisible zipper foot, stitch close to zipper teeth

Sew until mark for end of opening

① Remove basting and open zipper

If the zipper is too long, move the metal tab up to the mark for the end of opening and use pliers to pinch it into place. Cut off excess zipper tape.

4. Attach lining to skirt

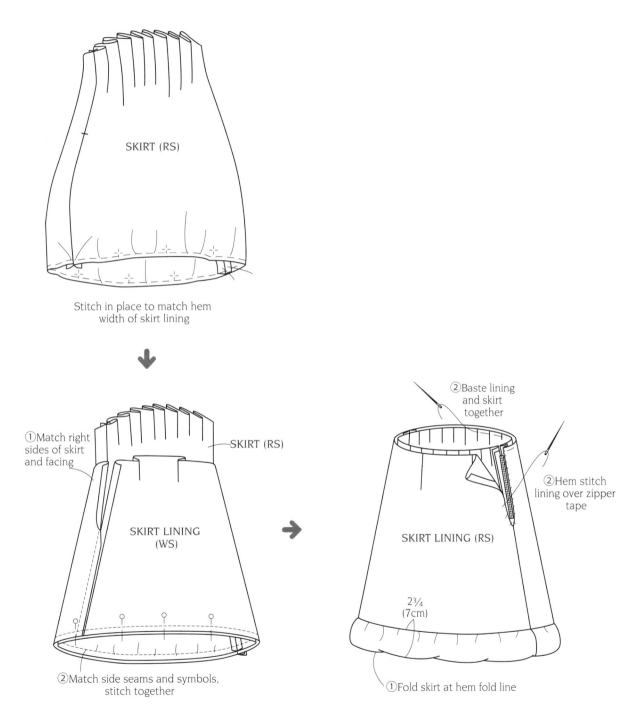

SKIRT (RS)

Stitch in place to match hem
width of skirt lining

①Match right
sides of skirt
and facing

SKIRT (RS)

SKIRT LINING
(WS)

②Match side seams and symbols,
stitch together

②Baste lining
and skirt
together

②Hem stitch
lining over zipper
tape

SKIRT LINING (RS)

2¾
(7cm)

①Fold skirt at hem fold line

5. Attach waist casing

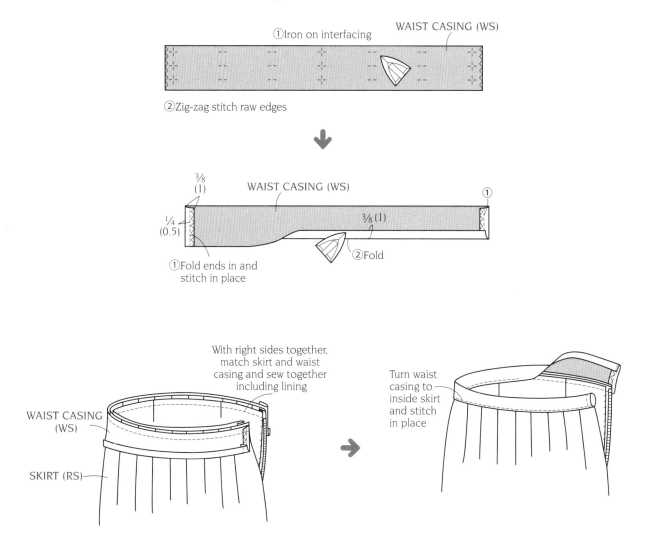

① Iron on interfacing

WAIST CASING (WS)

② Zig-zag stitch raw edges

³⁄₈ (1)

WAIST CASING (WS)

①

¹⁄₄ (0.5)

³⁄₈ (1)

① Fold ends in and stitch in place

② Fold

With right sides together, match skirt and waist casing and sew together including lining

WAIST CASING (WS)

SKIRT (RS)

Turn waist casing to inside skirt and stitch in place

6. Create waist tie and insert through casing

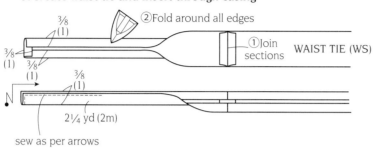

②Fold around all edges

①Join sections

WAIST TIE (WS)

³⁄₈ (1)

³⁄₈ (1)

³⁄₈ (1)

³⁄₈ (1)

N

2¼ yd (2m)

sew as per arrows

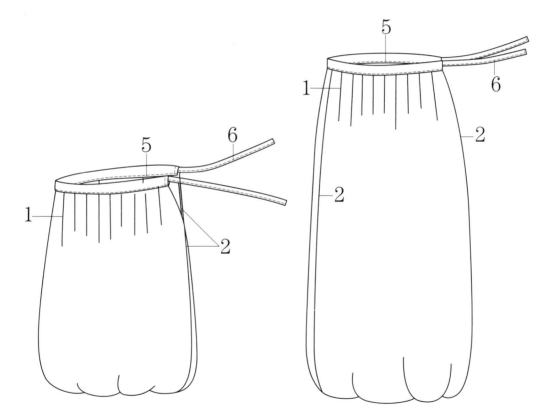

5

1

6

2

2

5

6

1

2

ℝ Skirt with Shirred Yoke and Lace Belt (photo→p.24-25)

MATERIALS

Fabric—double gauze dobby check washer 44 in (110cm)
  wide x 1⅔ yd (1.5m)
Iron-on interfacing—⅞ in (2cm) x 9 in (22cm)
1 x invisible zipper, 9 in (22cm) long
Hook and eye
Torchon lace ⅝ in (1.5cm) wide x3⅛ yd (2.8m)
Shirring elastic

SEWING STEPS

1. Sew right side, create shirring
2. Sew left side to opening and insert
   zipper (see p76)
3. Attach loops to waist
4. Create hem
5. Create belt
6. Attach hook and eye (see p63)

• Drafting and cutting layout (skirt)

Figures inside brackets show seam allowances.
Where not indicated, allow ⅜ in (1cm).

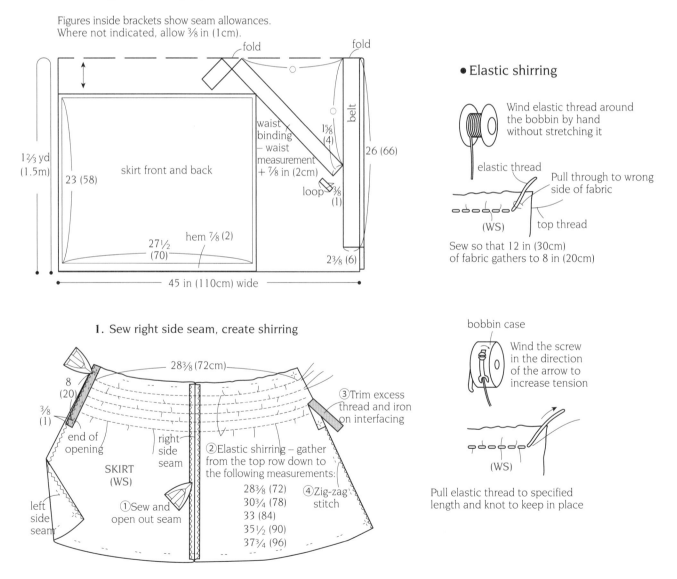

• Elastic shirring

Wind elastic thread around
the bobbin by hand
without stretching it

elastic thread

Pull through to wrong
side of fabric

top thread

(WS)

Sew so that 12 in (30cm)
of fabric gathers to 8 in (20cm)

fold

fold

belt

waist
binding
– waist
measurement
+ ⅞ in (2cm)

1⅝
(4)

26 (66)

loop ⅜
(1)

1⅔ yd
(1.5m)

23 (58)

skirt front and back

hem ⅞ (2)

27½
(70)

2⅜ (6)

45 in (110cm) wide

1. Sew right side seam, create shirring

28⅜ (72cm)

8
(20)

③Trim excess
thread and iron
on interfacing

⅜
(1)

end of
opening

right
side
seam

②Elastic shirring – gather
from the top row down to
the following measurements:

SKIRT
(WS)

left
side
seam

①Sew and
open out seam

④Zig-zag
stitch

28⅜ (72)
30¾ (78)
33 (84)
35½ (90)
37¾ (96)

bobbin case

Wind the screw
in the direction
of the arrow to
increase tension

(WS)

Pull elastic thread to specified
length and knot to keep in place

3. Attach loops and waist binding

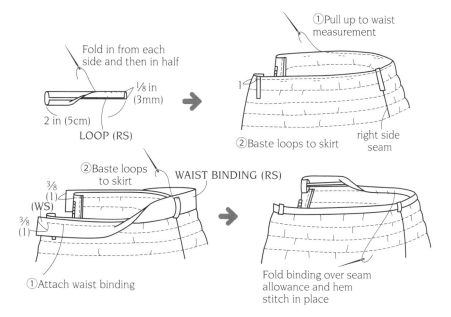

Fold in from each side and then in half

⅛ in (3mm)

2 in (5cm)

LOOP (RS)

① Pull up to waist measurement

② Baste loops to skirt

right side seam

② Baste loops to skirt

WAIST BINDING (RS)

⅜ (1)

(WS)

⅜ (1)

① Attach waist binding

Fold binding over seam allowance and hem stitch in place

5. Create belt

52 in (132cm) long

1⅛ (3)   BELT (RS)   fold line

1⅛ (3)

Stitch in place

lace ⅝ in (1.5cm) wide

⅜ (1)

⅜ (1)

(WS)

⅜ (1) Fold around all edges

① Fold along fold line

② Sew as per arrows

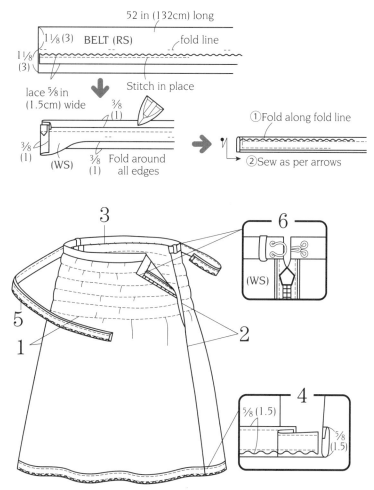

3

6

(WS)

5

1

2

4

⅝ (1.5)

⅝ (1.5)

S Linen Skirt with Cargo Pockets (photo→p.26)

MATERIALS

Fabric—linen 44 in (110cm) wide x 2⅛ yd (1.9m)
Iron-on interfacing 24 in (60cm) x 16 in (40cm)
1 x invisible zipper, 9 in (22cm) long
Hook and eye

SEWING STEPS

1. Sew sides
2. Attach pockets
3. Sew center back seam to opening and insert zipper (see p76)
4. Attach waist facing (see p67)
5. Create hem (see p67)
6. Attach belt loops
7. Attach hook and eye

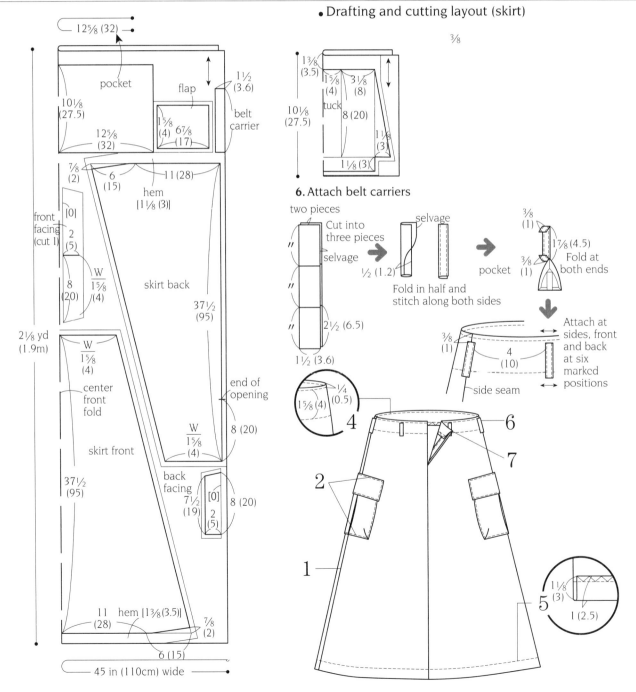

• Drafting and cutting layout (skirt)

2. Attach pockets

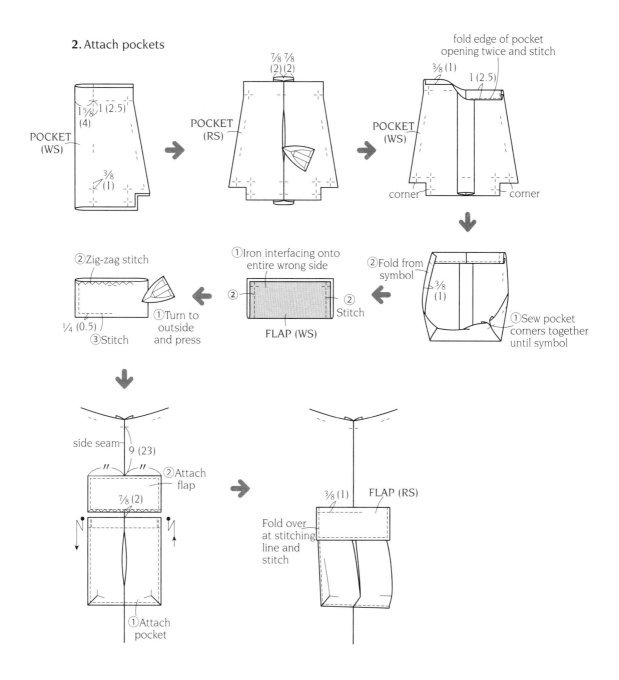

POCKET (WS)

1 5/8 (4) 1 (2.5) 3/8 (1)

POCKET (RS)

7/8 (2) 7/8 (2)

POCKET (WS)

fold edge of pocket opening twice and stitch

3/8 (1) 1 (2.5)

corner corner

②Fold from symbol

3/8 (1)

①Sew pocket corners together until symbol

①Iron interfacing onto entire wrong side

② ②Stitch

FLAP (WS)

②Zig-zag stitch

①Turn to outside and press

1/4 (0.5) ③Stitch

side seam 9 (23)

②Attach flap

7/8 (2)

①Attach pocket

3/8 (1) FLAP (RS)

Fold over at stitching line and stitch

⊤ Embroidered Skirt with Horizontal Tuck Pattern (photo→p.27)

MATERIALS
Fabric—44 in (112cm) wide x 2¾ yd (2.5m)
Embroidery thread—light green

SEWING STEPS
1. Create buttonholes for drawstring
2. Create pintucks
3. Sew side seams
4. Sew waist
5. Sew hem
6. Create drawstring and insert into casing
7. Embroider between tucks

● Drafting and cutting layout

Figures inside brackets show seam allowances.
Where not indicated, allow ⅜in (1cm).

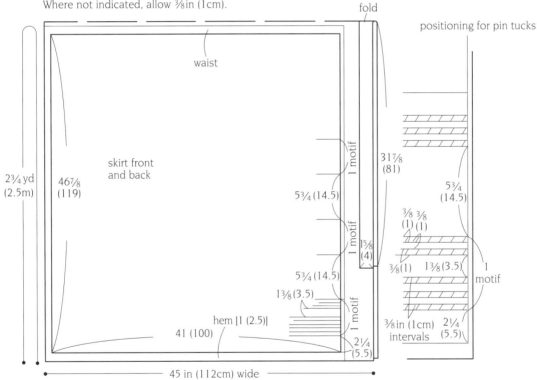

fold

positioning for pin tucks

waist

skirt front and back

2¾ yd (2.5m)

46⅞ (119)

1 motif

31⅞ (81)

5¾ (14.5)

5¾ (14.5)

⅜ ⅜ (1) (1)

1 motif

1⅝ (4)

⅜(1) 1⅜(3.5)

1 motif

5¾ (14.5)

1⅜ (3.5)

hem [1 (2.5)]

41 (100)

1 motif

2¼ (5.5)

⅜in (1cm) intervals

2¼ (5.5)

1 motif

45 in (112cm) wide

1. Create casing openings

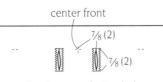

center front

⅞ (2)

⅞ (2)

Create as per buttonholes

2. Make pin tucks

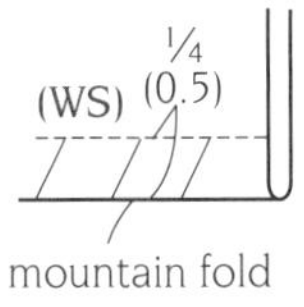

(WS)

¼ (0.5)

mountain fold

Diagonal lines indicate tucks. Make a mountain fold at the center of the tuck and sew ¼ in (0.5cm) along fold

embroidery guide (to scale)

french knot

¼ in (0.5cm)

⅝ (1.5)

satin stitch

2 in (5cm)

¼ in (0.5cm)

⅝ (1.5)

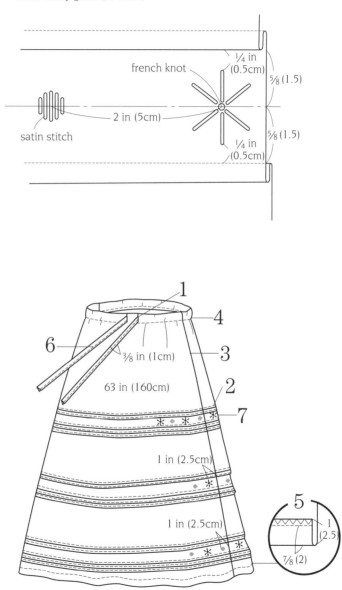

1

4

6

3

⅜ in (1cm)

63 in (160cm)

2

7

1 in (2.5cm)

1 in (2.5cm)

5

1 (2.5)

⅞ (2)

ⓤ Eight-button Skirt with Horizontal Stripe Sections (photo→p.28)

MATERIALS
Fabric—52 in (130cm) wide x 1 yd (90cm) [Bordeaux],
  ⅓ yd (30cm) [white], ⅔ yd (60cm) [purple]
Iron-on interfacing 24 in (60cm) x 16 (40cm)
Buttons—8 at ⅞ in (2cm) diameter

SEWING STEPS
1. Join upper, middle and lower sections and open out seams
2. Sew front left seam and stitch on outside (see p40)
3. Sew side seam to waist mark
4. Attach facing
5. Sew front right seam and stitch on outside (see p40)
6. Create hem (see p67)
7. Create buttonholes and attach buttons (see p63)

• Cutting layout

Figures inside brackets show seam allowances.
Where not indicated, allow ⅜ in (1cm).

• Drafting

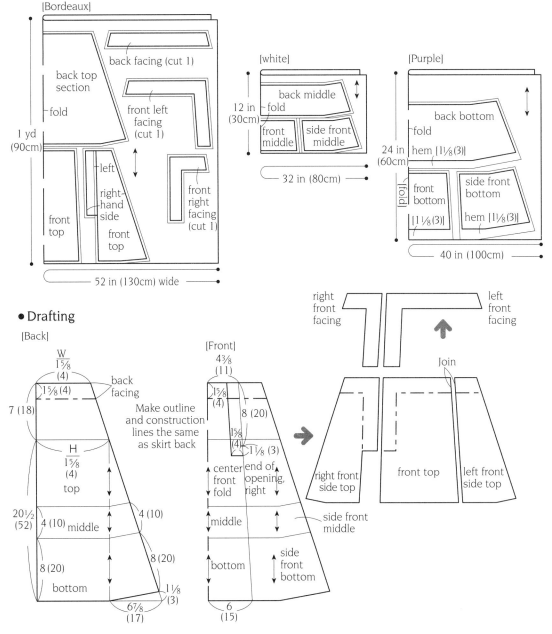

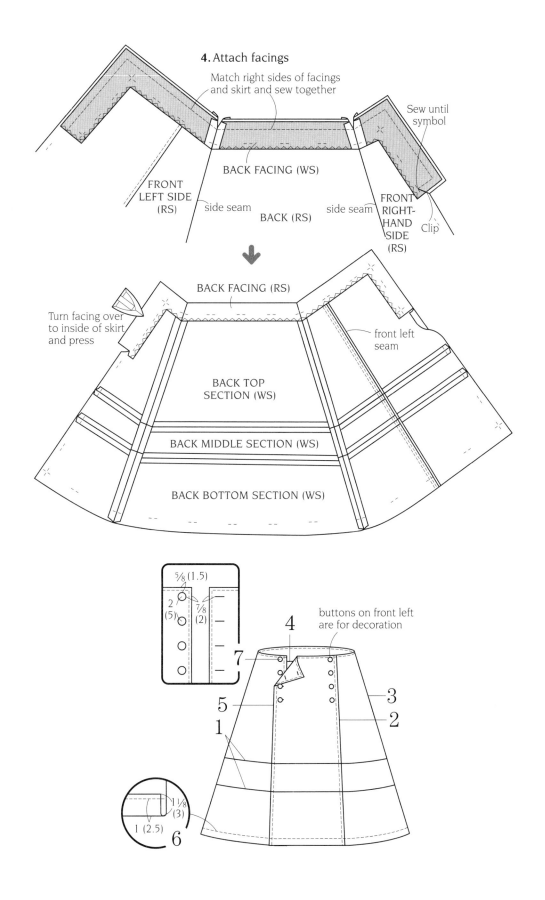

4. Attach facings

Match right sides of facings and skirt and sew together

Sew until symbol

BACK FACING (WS)

FRONT LEFT SIDE (RS)

side seam

BACK (RS)

side seam

FRONT RIGHT-HAND SIDE (RS)

Clip

BACK FACING (RS)

Turn facing over to inside of skirt and press

front left seam

BACK TOP SECTION (WS)

BACK MIDDLE SECTION (WS)

BACK BOTTOM SECTION (WS)

⅝ (1.5)

2 (5)

⅞ (2)

7

buttons on front left are for decoration

4

5

3

2

1

1⅛ (3)

1 (2.5)

6

ⓥ 8-panel Skirt In Three Colors (photo→p.29)

MATERIALS
52 in (130cm) wide x ⅞ yd (80cm) each of white,
  gray and light blue
Iron-on interfacing—2⅜ in (6cm) x 31½ in (80cm)
1 x invisible zipper, 9 in (22cm) long
Hook and eye

SEWING STEPS
1. Join the 18 panels and create pin tucks
2. Sew left side seam
3. Insert zipper (see p76)
4. Attach waistband (see p50)
5. Create hem (see p67)
6. Attach hook and eye (see p63)

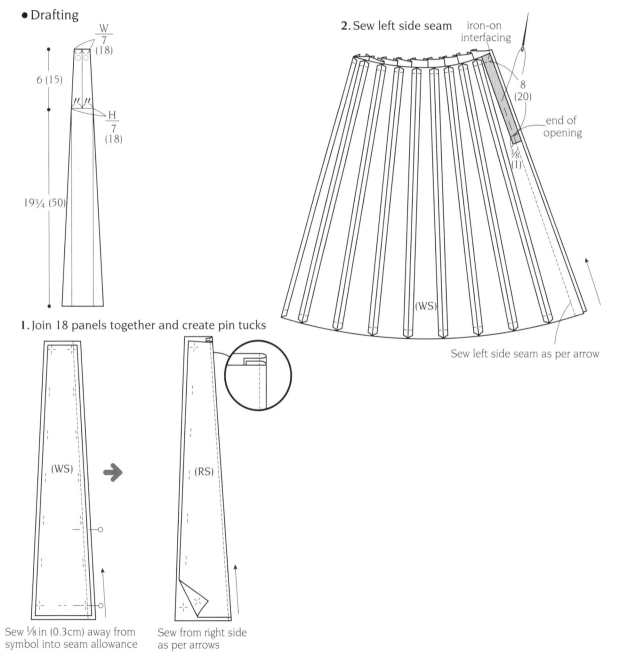

● Drafting

$\frac{W}{7}$ (18)

6 (15)

$\frac{H}{7}$ (18)

19¾ (50)

2. Sew left side seam

iron-on interfacing

8 (20)

end of opening

⅜ (1)

(WS)

Sew left side seam as per arrow

1. Join 18 panels together and create pin tucks

(WS)

(RS)

Sew ⅛ in (0.3cm) away from symbol into seam allowance

Sew from right side as per arrows

Sew 18 panels together in white, gray, light blue order

● Cutting layout

Figures inside brackets show seam allowances. Where not indicated, allow ⅜ in (1cm).

Cut 6 each of white, gray, light blue

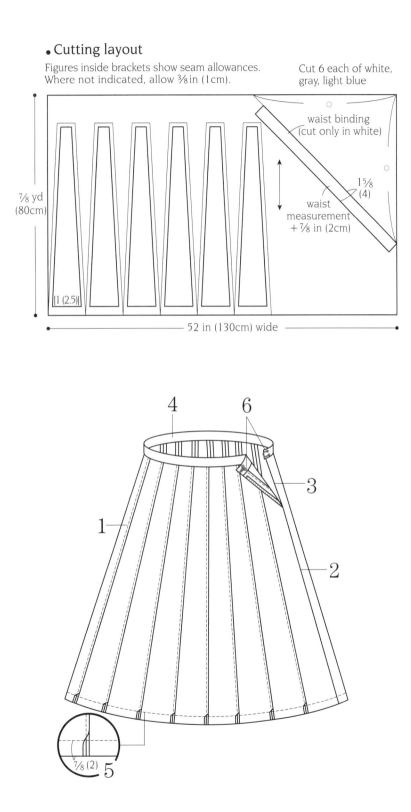

waist binding (cut only in white)

1⅝ (4)

waist measurement + ⅞ in (2cm)

⅞ yd (80cm)

1 (2.5)

52 in (130cm) wide

4   6

3

1

2

⅞ (2)   5

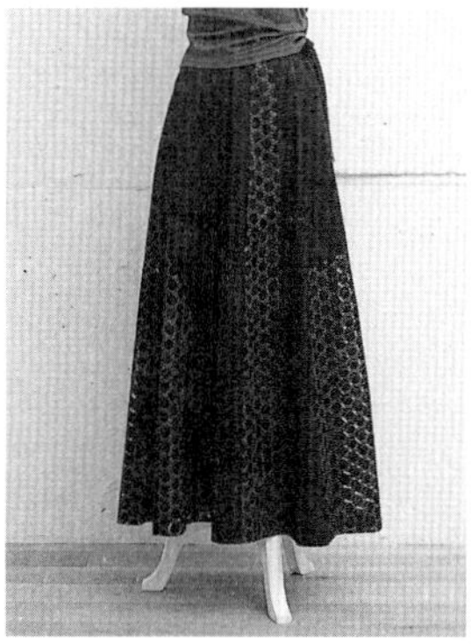

ⓦ Eight-panel Irregular Flare Skirt in Lace (photo→p.30-31)

MATERIALS

Fabric—lace 41 in (100cm) wide x 1¾ yd (1.6m)
Washable dobby—20 in (50cm) x 31½ in (80cm),
   lawn—25⅞ in (65cm) x 1⅛ yd (1m),
   seersucker—16 in (40cm) x 1⅛ yd (1m),
   check—24 in (60cm) x 31½ in (80cm)
Lining—Bemberg 36 in (92cm) wide x 2¼ yd (2m)
1 x zipper 8 in (20cm) long

SEWING STEPS

1. Join panels for skirt
2. Make lining
3. Sew left side seam of skirt and create hem (see p67)
4. Match skirt and lining and stitch together at left side opening
5. Insert zipper
6. Attach waistband (see p55)
7. Create waist cord and insert into casing

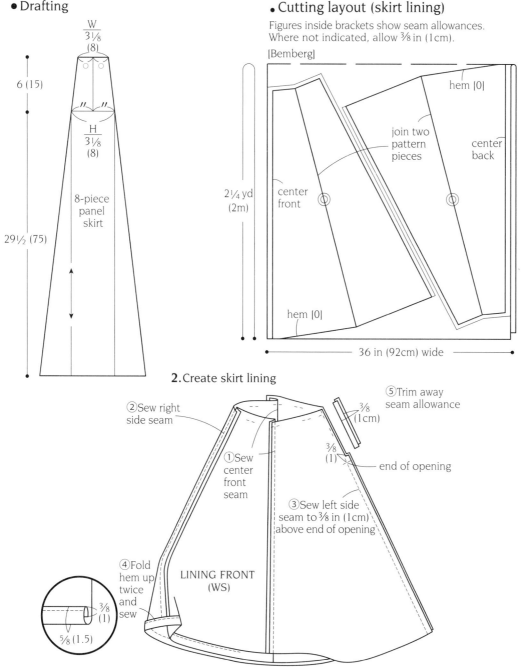

● Drafting

$\frac{W}{3⅛}$
(8)

6 (15)

$\frac{H}{3⅛}$
(8)

8-piece panel skirt

29½ (75)

● Cutting layout (skirt lining)

Figures inside brackets show seam allowances.
Where not indicated, allow ⅜ in (1cm).

[Bemberg]

hem [0]

join two pattern pieces

center back

center front

2¼ yd (2m)

hem [0]

36 in (92cm) wide

2. Create skirt lining

②Sew right side seam

⑤Trim away seam allowance

⅜ (1cm)

①Sew center front seam

⅜ (1)

end of opening

③Sew left side seam to ⅜ in (1cm) above end of opening

④Fold hem up twice and sew

LINING FRONT (WS)

⅜ (1)

⅝ (1.5)

● Cutting layout Draft skirt, waist and waist tie using diagrams below as a guide

1. Create casing openings

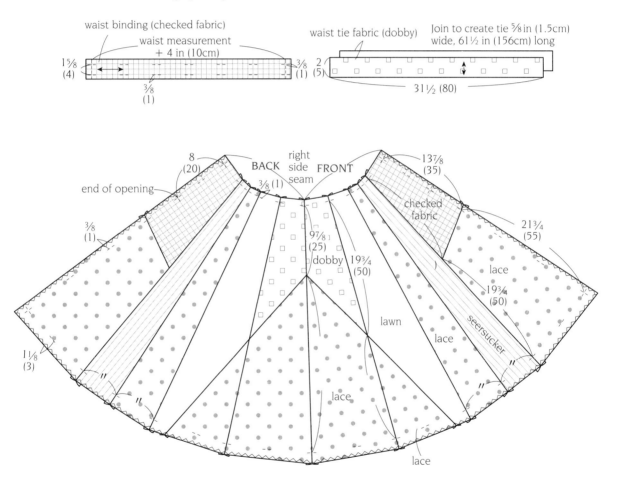

waist binding (checked fabric)
waist measurement + 4 in (10cm)
1⅝ (4)
⅜ (1)
⅜ (1)

waist tie fabric (dobby)
Join to create tie ⅝ in (1.5cm) wide, 61½ in (156cm) long
2 (5)
31½ (80)

8 (20)
end of opening
⅜ (1)
right side seam
BACK
FRONT
13⅞ (35)
⅜ (1)
checked fabric
9⅞ (25)
dobby
19¾ (50)
21¾ (55)
lace
19¾ (50)
lawn
lace
seersucker
1⅛ (3)
lace
lace

4. Match right sides of skirt and lining and sew left side opening

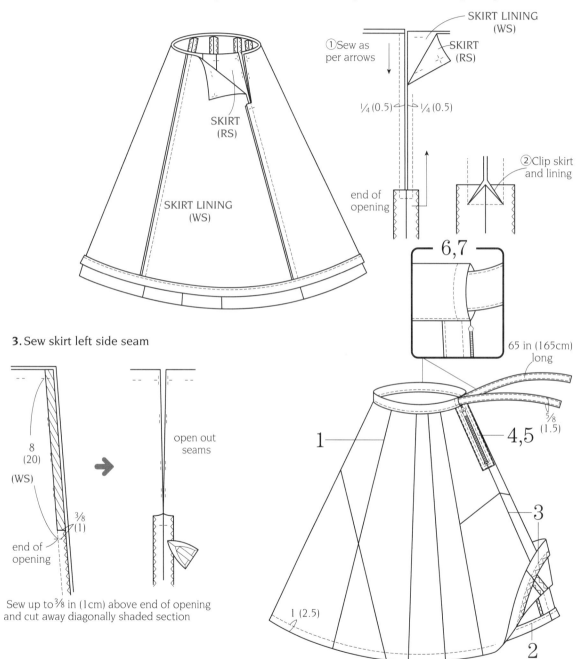

SKIRT LINING
(WS)

①Sew as
per arrows

SKIRT
(RS)

¼ (0.5) ¼ (0.5)

end of
opening

②Clip skirt
and lining

6,7

65 in (165cm)
long

⅝
(1.5)

1

4,5

3

1 (2.5)

2

SKIRT
(RS)

SKIRT LINING
(WS)

3. Sew skirt left side seam

8
(20)

(WS)

open out
seams

⅜
(1)

end of
opening

Sew up to ⅜ in (1cm) above end of opening
and cut away diagonally shaded section

5. Attach zipper

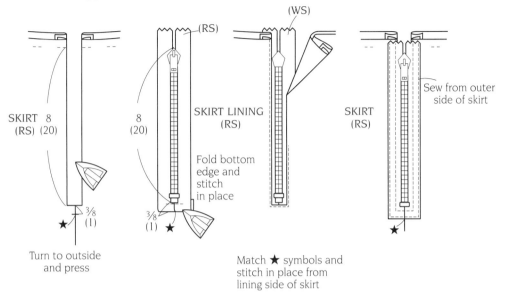

SKIRT 8
(RS) (20)

8
(20)

SKIRT LINING
(RS)

(RS)

(WS)

SKIRT
(RS)

Fold bottom
edge and
stitch
in place

³⁄₈
(1)

³⁄₈
(1)

★

★

★

Sew from outer
side of skirt

Turn to outside
and press

Match ★ symbols and
stitch in place from
lining side of skirt

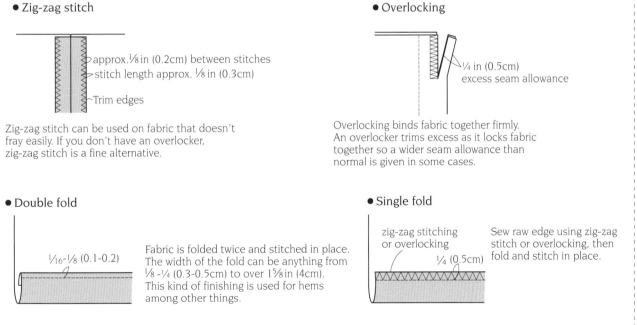

- Finishing off seam allowances

- Zig-zag stitch

approx.⅛ in (0.2cm) between stitches
stitch length approx. ⅛ in (0.3cm)

Trim edges

Zig-zag stitch can be used on fabric that doesn't
fray easily. If you don't have an overlocker,
zig-zag stitch is a fine alternative.

- Overlocking

¼ in (0.5cm)
excess seam allowance

Overlocking binds fabric together firmly.
An overlocker trims excess as it locks fabric
together so a wider seam allowance than
normal is given in some cases.

- Double fold

¹⁄₁₆-⅛ (0.1-0.2)

Fabric is folded twice and stitched in place.
The width of the fold can be anything from
⅛ -¼ (0.3-0.5cm) to over 1⅝ in (4cm).
This kind of finishing is used for hems
among other things.

- Single fold

zig-zag stitching
or overlocking

¼ (0.5cm)

Sew raw edge using zig-zag
stitch or overlocking, then
fold and stitch in place.

Sewing Terms

Backing—fabric is backed with separate fabric to strengthen it or create thickness or body. The fabric and the backing fabric are treated as one layer of material.

W (waist)—the waist or area around it, between the ribcage and hips. The narrowest section is called the waistline. In this book, "W" refers to the nude waist measurement plus about 1⅝ (4cm), that is, the finished waist measurement.

Shirring—after a line of machine stitching is sewn, bobbin threads are pulled to create volume in the material. Shirring elastic is usually used for the bobbin thread. See p80.

Dart—used to fit fabric to a form, a dart is made by pinching in a small amount of fabric to reduce fullness, tapering it to a point.

Tuck—a stitched fold of fabric. The term can refer to the stitched fold of fabric used when creating an architectural silhouette, or to the act of creating the fold. A tuck can aid in freedom of movement in a garment or to add a decorative touch. The edge of a tuck is not stitched down or concealed.

Match right sides—join two pieces of fabric so the right (or outer) sides are facing each other (opposite of "match wrong sides")

Seam allowance—the amount of extra fabric required when sections of a garment are joined by a seam. It is added on around the outside when a pattern is cut out, and is concealed inside the finished garment.

Panel—extra fabric inserted vertically into garments such as skirts, either as part of the design or for decoration.

H (hip)—the area around the hip and buttocks. A hip measurement should be taken at the widest part with the tape measure lying flat against the body. In this book, H refers to the finished hip measurement – that is, the nude hip measurement with about 1⅝ (4cm) added on for ease.

Open seam—to open out the seam by bringing the seam allowance to lie on either side of the center. A flattened seam is when both sides of the seam allowance are ironed together to lie on one side.

Symbols Used

Finished garment

_____

– –   – –   – –   – –   – –

Measurement division line (○,
" are also used in some cases)

Right angle line. This serves
as a guide when drafting patterns

Fabric fold line

——   ——   ——   ——

Symbol for matching pattern pieces.
Use to match pieces to form into new pattern

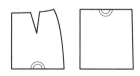

Grain line.
Place fabric so grain runs parallel to this line.

Facing line

— · — · — · — · — · —

Matching symbol. Position these
symbols together to match up
two pieces of fabric correctly

Tuck. The diagonal line shows the
direction of the tuck. In this diagram,
the left side goes on top.

Published in 2014 by Tuttle Publishing, an imprint of Periplus Editions (HK) Ltd.

www.tuttlepublishing.com

ISBN 978-4-8053-1307-7

CHOKUSENNUI NANONI KIREI NA SILHOUETTE NO SKIRT
by Sato WATANABE.
© 2006 by Sato WATANABE
All rights reserved.
Original Japanese edition published in 2006 by Kawade Shobo Shinsha. Ltd.
    Publishers, Tokyo
English translation rights arranged with Kawade Shobo Shinsha. Ltd.
    Publishers through Japan UNI Agency, Inc., Tokyo
English Translation © 2014 Periplus Editions (HK) Ltd.

Art direction and design: Masami Furuta
Photography: sai
Instructions (words): Yumiko Yoshimoto (a-f, h-j, l-m, p-w),
    Rie Niitsuma (g, k, n-o)
Illustrations: Noriko Hachimonji, Mamiko Kobayashi
Sewing trials: Mieko Yumoto, Utako Imai, Mitsuko Isogaya,
    Rie Niitsuma, Kumiko Ogawa, Fumiko Koyanagi, Yorie
Editing: Atsuko Sakamoto

Translated from Japanese by Leeyong Soo

Distributed by

North America, Latin America & Europe
Tuttle Publishing
364 Innovation Drive, North Clarendon, VT 05759-9436 U.S.A.
Tel: 1 (802) 773-8930
Fax: 1 (802) 773-6993
info@tuttlepublishing.com
www.tuttlepublishing.com

Japan
Tuttle Publishing
Yaekari Building, 3rd Floor, 5-4-12 Osaki, Shinagawa-ku, Tokyo 141 0032
Tel: (81) 3 5437-0171
Fax: (81) 3 5437-0755
sales@tuttle.co.jp
www.tuttle.co.jp

Asia Pacific
Berkeley Books Pte. Ltd.
61 Tai Seng Avenue #02-12, Singapore 534167
Tel: (65) 6280-1330
Fax: (65) 6280-6290
inquiries@periplus.com.sg
www.periplus.com

Printed in Singapore   1402TW
17 16 15 14   6 5 4 3 2 1

TUTTLE PUBLISHING® is a registered trademark of Tuttle Publishing,
a division of Periplus Editions (HK) Ltd.

The Tuttle Story
"Books to Span the East and West"

Many people are surprised to learn that the world's largest publisher of books on Asia had its humble beginnings in the tiny American state of Vermont. The company's founder, Charles E. Tuttle, belonged to a New England family steeped in publishing.

Tuttle's father was a noted antiquarian dealer in Rutland, Vermont. Young Charles honed his knowledge of the trade working in the family bookstore, and later in the rare books section of Columbia University Library. His passion for beautiful books—old and new—never wavered throughout his long career as a bookseller and publisher.

After graduating from Harvard, Tuttle enlisted in the military and in 1945 was sent to Tokyo to work on General Douglas MacArthur's staff. He was tasked with helping to revive the Japanese publishing industry, which had been utterly devastated by the war. When his tour of duty was completed, he left the military, married a talented and beautiful singer, Reiko Chiba, and in 1948 began several successful business ventures.

To his astonishment, Tuttle discovered that postwar Tokyo was actually a book-lover's paradise. He befriended dealers in the Kanda district and began supplying rare Japanese editions to American libraries. He also imported American books to sell to the thousands of GIs stationed in Japan. By 1949, Tuttle's business was thriving, and he opened Tokyo's very first English-language bookstore in the Takashimaya Department Store in Ginza, to great success. Two years later, he began publishing books to fulfill the growing interest of foreigners in all things Asian.

Though a westerner, Tuttle was hugely instrumental in bringing a knowledge of Japan and Asia to a world hungry for information about the East. By the time of his death in 1993, he had published over 6,000 books on Asian culture, history and art—a legacy honored by Emperor Hirohito in 1983 with the "Order of the Sacred Treasure," the highest honor Japan can bestow upon a non-Japanese.

The Tuttle company today maintains an active backlist of some 1,500 titles, many of which have been continuously in print since the 1950s and 1960s—a great testament to Charles Tuttle's skill as a publisher. More than 60 years after its founding, Tuttle Publishing is more active today than at any time in its history, still inspired by Charles Tuttle's core mission—to publish fine books to span the East and West and provide a greater understanding of each.